Contents

Introduction

Positive action in employment is about making equal opportunity policies work. Over the past ten years, more and more employers have turned their attention to equal opportunities issues:

- are we employing women and black people?
- are we promoting women and black people?
- are our employment policies in keeping with equality laws?

In explaining positive action and describing some of the initiatives that have been taken, we intend to show how employers can ensure that they guarantee equal opportunities for all their workforce, in accordance with the law; and how Trade Unions and staff associations can agitate for, and negotiate, good equal opportunity practices.

Positive action is frequently confused with positive discrimination. Even government ministers have been heard to proclaim that positive action will mean discrimination against white people or against men. However, there is an important distinction between the two approaches. Positive discrimination consists of setting quotas, and therefore using discrimination at the point of recruitment to meet these targets. This is unlawful in the UK. Positive action, on the other hand, can involve a multitude of things, but is essentially about educating and advising employers and training bodies as to the requirements of the Equality Legislation; setting goals for management; devising strategies and timetables for achieving these goals; and ensuring that the law is enforced. There is considerable evidence to show that many employers are either ignorant of these requirements, or are determined to ignore them.

If an employing body with a predominance of male employees takes active steps to ensure that its job vacancies are widely-publicised, that women are given every chance and encouragement to apply, and that job requirements reflect a commitment to equality of opportunity, this is *not* discrimination against men, but an effort to correct an existing imbalance and to counter the effects of past discrimination against women.

What is Positive Action?

The Sex Discrimination Act and the Equal Pay Act, put into effect in 1975, made it unlawful to treat women less favourably than men in education, training and employment. The Race Relations Act of 1976 similarly outlawed racial discrimination.

These pieces of legislation were the culmination of years of campaigning by the women's and the trade union movements and by Black people, and although few people imagined that they would in themselves guarantee equal opportunity in training or at work, there was certainly the hope that they would form a solid legal basis from which to develop and fight for good practices.

This book sets out to explain and describe what those good practices might be; how they can be negotiated; and which forms of positive action and equal opportunities policies are the most effective. We are primarily concerned with positive action for women in paid work. However, where relevant, we will refer to initiatives in the areas of education and training.

We will also refer to the Race Relations Act and the Disabled Persons Act inasmuch as they provide women workers with further legislative protection.

The Equality Legislation

The Equal Pay Act (EqPA) covers contractual issues, terms and conditions of employment, and wage rates. The Sex Discrimination Act (SDA) covers employment practice, policy and training. The Race Relations Act (RRA) is roughly equivalent to the Sex Discrimination Act, but it also covers wage rates and contracts, thus combining these provisions in a single piece of legislation.

The SDA introduces the concept of indirect discrimination: that is, treating a woman less favourably than a man would have been treated, or making stipulations which men can more easily meet. Thus, if a rule or requirement can be shown to have a disproportionate impact on women; to affect women adversely; and to be unjustifiable; then it is unlawful. The RRA also contains the concept of indirect discrimination.

One of the drawbacks of the EqPA is that women cannot claim indirect discrimination or compare their wages or other contractual terms with those of a 'notional man'. However, amendments to the EqPA which allow women to bring claims for equal pay for work of equal value took effect in January 1984, as a result of a European Court of Justice judgment which stated that UK legislation did not fully comply with the EEC Directive on equal pay. The Equal Value Amendment has been slow in enforcement. In its first year of operation, only 23 cases reached industrial tribunals, and it was 10 months before a case was successful.

The Equal Opportunities Commission (EOC) was set up in 1975, with a statutory duty to monitor the SDA and the EqPA and to promote equality of opportunity between men and women. Similarly, the Commission for Racial Equality (CRE) was set up to promote racial equality. It was intended that both Commissions be responsible for enforcing the laws; indeed, it must have been apparent to those drafting the legislation that it was inadequate, because the Commissions were enjoined to keep the Acts under review, and where necessary to report to Parliament with recommendations for change. However, they were given no executive powers to effect any changes. The CRE has marginally greater statutory powers than the EOC, but large constraints restrict the work of both Commissions.

The EOC was originally given power under the SDA to carry out Formal Investigations into employing organisations. There was no requirement that it believed the law was being broken. This power was rescinded when the equivalent provision in the RRA, passed a year later, included such a requirement.

So although a need for the power to investigate employers was initially conceived as a necessary part of the sex equality legislation, neither Commission is now able to use its investigative powers to promote good employment practices — merely to remedy bad ones. Active reinforcement of the equality legislation has been restricted in this way. Where discriminatory practices have been uncovered by an Industrial Tribunal (IT), the tribunal has no powers to order that the discriminating body takes positive measures to ensure that it avoids further discrimination.

In addition, women who win a discrimination case are not automatically entitled to reinstatement if they have been sacked: indeed, one woman winning a case does not even guarantee a change of practice by which other women employees, who are known to have been treated in the same discriminatory way, are compensated or treated fairly. Women in the USA are in a better position: Class Actions (see p. 106) enable all the women in one company to take action together.

Positive Approaches to Equality

In spite of their shortcomings, the SDA and the RRA both take note of the principle of positive action. In order to counteract the effects of past discrimination, they stipulate that measures to promote equality of opportunity must be actively pursued. However there are markedly different approaches to the introduction of positive action programmes into the workplace.

Positive Action specifically allowed under the SDA

Sections 47, 48 and 49 of the SDA make provision for positive action in the following areas:

1. *Training Bodies* — The Manpower Services Commission, the Training Services Division, the Employment Services Agency and Industry Training Boards are permitted to take positive action in certain circumstances outlined below.

Where it appears to one of these training bodies that, at any time during the preceding 12 months no women, or very few women, have been engaged in a particular kind of work, it is entitled to encourage women to do that work, to provide special training for women only, or to limit access to training to women. This may be done at a national level, or, if women are under-represented in a field of work in one part of the country, positive action may be taken in that area alone.

These training bodies may make provisions to train individuals who are in special need because of the time they have spent discharging domestic or family responsibilities. In other words, it is legal to provide special training for women returning to work after a period at home looking after their children.

Other training bodies can also offer special training facilities, provided they are officially designated for the purpose by the Secretary of State. (See p. 9.)

2. *Employers* — Where a particular type of work has been done mainly or wholly by men at any time over the preceding 12 months,

an employer may encourage women to apply for that work, and provide them with special training for it.

3. *Trade Unions, employers' organisations and professional associations* — If at any time over the last 12 months no women, or relatively few women, have been members of one of these organisations, it can take steps to encourage them to join. If no woman, or comparatively few women have, at any time in the last 12 months, held a post of any kind in the organisation, special steps may be taken to encourage women to apply for the post and to provide training so that they are qualified to hold it. For example, this enables Trade Unions to hold special shop steward training courses for women.

If women are under-represented on elected bodies within any one of these organisations, an appropriate number of seats for women may be reserved, or created (by co-option, election or otherwise). It is not lawful, however, to restrict voting for certain seats to women only, or to use other such means to ensure that more women are elected.

The difference between Positive Action and Positive Discrimination

The Sex Discrimination Act prohibits discrimination in favour of women at the point of selection. This means that while steps can be taken by employers or training bodies to ensure that women apply for jobs and are qualified to do them, when it comes to hiring people to do the job the best candidate must be selected irrespective of gender. Women are only to be assisted so that they can compete equally with men. Thus they are compensated for the societal discrimination they have experienced but not favoured over equally-qualified men. (See also 'The difference between *quotas* and *goals and timetables*', p. 110.)

Trade Unions can encourage women to put themselves forward as shop stewards or other officials, and they can hold special meetings and training sessions to equip women for these positions, but they cannot lawfully appoint women to these positions in preference to better qualified men.

Positive Action specifically allowed under the RRA

As well as permitting positive action for ethnic minority people in the same ways that the SDA permits positive action for women, the RRA places a duty on local authorities to ensure that they

5

perform their various functions 'with due regard to the need to eliminate unlawful racial discrimination and to promote equality of opportunity and good relations'. (Section 71, RRA.)

It is in the light of s.71 that some local authorities have incorporated equal opportunities stipulations into their agreements with outside contractors (see Contracts Compliance, p. 77). Although there is no equivalent requirement in the SDA, local authorities have in many cases understood s.71 as placing a general duty upon them to re-examine their record on equal opportunities, and to review employment and other practices across the board. However, the omission of a clause equivalent to s.71 from the SDA can only be seen as a failure in the drafting of the legislation; and indeed the Commission for Racial Equality, amongst others, has recommended that s.71 itself should have a wider remit.

Whilst s.71 *places a duty* on local authorities with regard to racial equality, it provides no guidelines as to how these duties should be carried out. It is inevitably a virtually unenforceable part of the RRA, and indeed numerous local authorities would appear to have ignored it completely. Local authorities who have tackled racial inequality through their contracts compliance policies have found that they are open to legal challenge, and indeed new legislation is being drafted which may render equal opportunities clauses in contracts compliance policies unlawful (see Contracts Compliance, p. 81).

Local authorities have also responded to s.71 by setting up Equal Opportunities and Ethnic Minorities Committees, and have established their own guidelines for these committees. Again this has been an individual policy matter rather than a self-evident requirement of s.71. There is also no reference in s.71 as to how the duties outlined should be financed: although legal challenges to local authorities' expenditure on equal opportunities programmes have not presented major problems, there has been an extraordinary level of media antipathy where local authorities have taken initiatives.

Furthermore, the duties outlined in s.71 are restricted to local authorities. There is no specific reference anywhere in the RRA to other public bodies, or to the disposing of public money which is carried out by them. Public and publicly-funded bodies by their nature have a particular kind of public accountability; but local authorities do not have a special function of law enforcement or social control which warrants this singling out. It is every bit as important that institutions such as the Police Force, the jobcentres and the Health Service should have their responsibilities defined by the Equality Legislation.

The Disabled Persons Acts

The Disabled Persons (Employment) Act 1944, which was amended in 1958, is unique in that it actually obliges employers to discriminate in favour of people who are registered disabled. Under the Act, employers with a workforce of more than 20 people are required to employ a quota of 3% registered disabled people. It is an offence to employ an able-bodied person in preference if the employer is not already employing the quota of disabled people, and an offence to refuse to produce detailed records on the make-up of the workforce on request. An employer who has tried and failed to meet the quota can get certification to this effect from the Manpower Services Commission, which is responsible for enforcing this law. The sanction carried by failure to meet the quota is prosecution in the Magistrates' Court.

This legislative attempt to help a disadvantaged minority is striking only for its lack of enforcement. A report by the Low Pay Unit showed that even where a firm is found to be in breach of the Act, it is unlikely to face prosecution. Fines have been minimal in those few cases which have reached this stage.

Further difficulties in enforcement arise with the registering of disabled people. For the purposes of employment, this is carried out by the Department of Employment and the Department of Health and Social Security. In theory every school-leaver with a disability will be registered disabled on leaving school, for a period of 5 years; after this time there will be a review and a decision will be made as to re-registration. In reality, however, after the initial registration it is up to each individual to seek re-registration.

Many people with disabilities are reluctant to do this – not only because it carries no noticeable benefits, but frequently because it can work to an individual's disadvantage in the job market.

Thus it becomes clear that a legislative framework for equal opportunity is not, in itself, adequate. Enforcement is essential if any legislation is to have an impact on workplace practice.

Building on the Equality Legislation

1. Positive Action to enforce the law

Many local authorities have taken steps to ensure that they are conforming both to the letter and spirit of the equality laws. Some, however, have gone further than this, and have actively promoted equal opportunities. The Acts do not require an employer to produce a policy for equal opportunity, nor do they give guidelines for assuring that opportunities are equal. The law does not impose specific requirements on employers to show that they are complying with it; and there is evidence to show that many employers still have no clear understanding of the basic provisions of the law.

CONTRACTS COMPLIANCE is one means of educating employers about the law. It will be explained more fully on p. 77.

GRANT AID TO THE VOLUNTARY SECTOR is another springboard local authorities can use to promote equal opportunity. Grant aid is in itself a way to provide support to, for example, women's employment projects, thus financing the promotion of equal opportunities. However, a local authority can also build positive action into its grant-awarding system. For example, the Greater London Council set up a thorough checking mechanism to ensure that agencies which it funded were both aware of the GLC's policy on equal opportunities, and were encouraged to institute their own policies. Agencies were monitored at various stages to ensure that they were mindful of equal opportunities both as employers and as providers of public services:

1. When a voluntary organisation filled in an application for funding, it had to answer questions as to the ways in which its work would benefit different sections of the community, such as women, people with disabilities, and ethnic minority communities.
2. A condition attached to grant-aid by the GLC was that the funded agency undertook to comply with the Council's equal opportunities policy when it accepted the grant.
3. Grant officers then monitored individual grants to satisfy themselves that all the conditions of payment had been complied with. Funded groups were required to produce a report on their work every 6 months, and also to inform the GLC about any changes in personnel. Where it appeared to the grant officers that a group was not fulfilling its equal opportunities policy, active support and assistance was available to broaden its approach.

The GLC's equal opportunities policy for voluntary groups encompassed both personnel procedures and the public functions of the group, i.e. its provision of services; and the purpose of the policy was to ensure that voluntary organisations understood, and operated, fair employment practices. Thus, although the Council did not necessarily require a group to analyse its workforce, it did expect it to employ staff who would have an awareness of equal opportunity issues, and who could be representative of the community they aimed to service.

4. The GLC also issued general guidelines on equal opportunities: for example, its Ethnic Minorities Unit produced a booklet for employers on how to avoid discriminating on the grounds of race.

As well as issuing guidelines and codes of practice on equal opportunities, some local authorities have held public meetings and workshops to explain to grant-aided groups how they can set up frameworks for equal opportunities and positive action, and to promote wider discussion of the issues.

2. Provision for special needs

Sections 47 and 48 of the SDA specifically permit training bodies and employers to make available facilities for training people who are 'in special need' (see p. 4).

Training bodies other than the MSC, Industry Training Boards and other named state training agencies have to seek designation from the Secretary of State in order to run this special training, although the 1986 Sex Discrimination Bill proposes to remove this requirement. There are currently approximately 150 bodies offering training to women under such designation. Of these, some are offering a wide range of courses, or long-term courses in specific crafts or skills. For example, East Leeds Women's Workshop has Section 47 designation to run women-only courses in carpentry and electronics. Others, like the London Business School, are reserving places and scholarships for women. However, a discouraging number of training agencies are using their special designation simply to run introductory courses, 'de-mystification' and taster courses, and 'self-development' workshops, for as little as 2½ days.

Equally, there is little evidence to suggest that employers have leapt at the opportunity to train women to fill their vacancies. A 1978 EOC survey of 441 employers revealed that only 7 had sought to exercise this option. This was in the main to provide management training for women employees. (Many of the Metropolitan authorities, such as London, Manchester and Merseyside, subsequently took positive action for their employees.)

There are also pitfalls in the concept of 'special needs' training provision: a training body or employer may cater for 'special needs' at the expense of scrutinising its usual recruitment practices. The

9

MSC for example has run courses specifically designed for women. Deptford Skillcentre, in South East London, offers a 10 week women-only 'taster' course in the various building trades, enabling trainees to gain some experience before undertaking a standard course in one trade. The course has been established on the basis that women are under-represented on Skillcentre building courses, and are unlikely to have had previous experience, but it is conceived as a temporary measure, designed to bridge the period between the introduction of the equality legislation and the eventual advent of full equality of opportunity. Successful completion of the course does not in itself assure women of a place on a full-term course. In fact it is not unknown for women to have been refused full training on the basis of their performance on a short course which is not supposed to be assessed.

Moreover, this provision does not in itself incorporate efforts to overhaul the methods of recruitment onto regular skills training courses, or to ensure that they do not discriminate; and despite the existence of such introductory courses, there has been no increase in the numbers of women going on to full craft training in Skillcentres – this figure is currently a mere 3%. This may be influenced by the lack of effective outreach advertising under the positive action sections of the Act.

3. Desegregating work

There is no doubt that employers discriminate against women for certain types of jobs. In the construction trades, and in many professions, employers either do not hire women, or do not promote them above the lowest grades; and women have not had access to training in many fields up until very recently. Some employers have already taken positive measures to desegregate labour – to encourage women into traditional 'men's jobs' and the reverse. Notable examples of such employers are local authorities through contracts compliance equal opportunities policies and also through their own hiring practices. Hackney Council, amongst others, has employed staff to tour local schools to encourage girls to consider non-traditional training. Many Council Direct Labour Organisations (building departments, or DLOs) have changed their apprentice requirements so that opportunities to train are not restricted to school leavers. This has resulted in more take-up of training by women, largely because slightly older women have more confidence to break conventions and train in male-dominated trades.

4. Re-evaluating women's work

Positive action to ensure that women get employed in non-traditional jobs, or have better opportunities for career advancement, is not in itself enough to improve the status of women at work. The relatively low rates of pay for jobs which are traditionally done by women cannot be attributed to the low value of the work: men's jobs are not, in their nature, necessarily more useful. The discrepancy in pay has to do with traditional assumptions about women and work, particularly the widespread underestimation of women workers' financial contribution to the support of dependents, and with the fact that male workers have been better organised and therefore in a stronger position to negotiate better pay and conditions.

There are numerous examples to show that as more and more women enter a field of employment, salaries gradually fall there relative to other jobs. Before the equal pay legislation this was a straightforward exercise; now it is done by gradually removing some of the more challenging aspects of the job and thereby reducing its status. Over the last century this is what has happened to many clerical and secretarial jobs: they were originally prestigious jobs with good prospects, but as increasing numbers of women entered an expanding employment sector, the wages were increasingly depressed and the opportunities for advancement blocked. A more recent example of the development of this pattern is in the computing industry. As the industry has grown and become more sophisticated, women have been segregated into the 'non-technical' sides of the work, which have themselves expanded; and as technological processes have become more familiar and straightforward, they have been simplified and labelled 'women's work'.

Thus it is clear that a positive action programme which does not include provisions for ensuring equal pay for work of equal value, will be ineffective; women will not get better pay simply because they enter the same jobs for which men have received high wages. And if the women entering new fields of employment are a mere trailblazing handful, this will not affect women's pay and status in general.

Similarly, it is important that an equal value scheme includes a positive action programme: if employers are forced to pay higher wages for 'women's work', there is nothing to prevent them hiring only, or mostly men, and the result will be that women lose jobs.

Clearly, if the true value of women's work were recognised, they would be paid more. In the long term this might be achieved by increasing the level of women's participation in the unions. We investigate positive measures for encouraging women's TU activity on p. 83. Some jobs could be up-graded by making use of the existing job evaluation and statutory machinery.

(a) Job Evaluation

The Equal Pay Act requires that women should receive equal pay with men where they are doing the same job; and the Equal Value Amendment further requires that they should receive equal pay for work of equal value.

The 'value' of a job is determined for the purposes of the EqPA, by a job evaluation scheme, which can be conducted in a number of different ways. Broadly speaking, job evaluation is an attempt to assess objectively the relative value of different jobs within an organisation. Employers are not required to undertake job evaluation, but an equal value claim to an Industrial Tribunal may be resolved by such a scheme.

According to the EqPA, the value of each job must be assessed analytically; that is, according to different job elements, which will include such factors as the effort, skill, responsibility and working conditions of the job. The findings of a job evaluation scheme can be challenged on the basis that it was discriminatory; for example, many schemes have attached greater weight to job factors more likely to feature in men's jobs, such as strength, and less weight to factors particular to women's jobs, such as dexterity.

Job evaluation schemes can also be challenged if they are out of date, that is, if the claimant's job or that of the man or men with which she is comparing it has changed significantly; or if the schemes are based on inaccurate information.

Clearly, so long as a job evaluation scheme does not undervalue the skills particular to women's jobs, it can serve to upgrade women's work; but it needs to be controlled by management *and* the union; and on the union side, women representing women's sections of the workforce need to be involved. Union representatives need to be properly trained so that they understand the scheme from the start.

Most schemes are tailor-made for the particular workplace in order to produce a result which is broadly acceptable to management and unions. At the very outset, when the scheme is being designed, it is important for the union representatives to scrutinise the criteria which are being proposed and ensure that they are not biased in favour of 'men's jobs'.

Two recent judgments illustrate how job evaluation can affect women's pay.

The Ford Sewing-machinists. In 1966 a job evaluation scheme was introduced into the Ford Motor Company. Five job characteristics were measured in each job:

1. Accuracy required
2. Knowledge of the process
3. Ability to visualise shapes
4. Appreciation of detail
5. Paced muscular effort.

The (women) sewing machinists were recommended for a skilled production grade, but in the event were put on a lower grade. This resulted in a historic pay strike, but it took 17 years to win the dispute about grading. The 1970 Equal Pay Act failed to secure a fair grading because the women machinists were not doing 'the same or like work' as any men on higher grades. In other words, there were no men doing the same job with whom they could compare themselves. Thus the Equal Pay legislation had completely failed to confront the issues of job segregation, and the undervaluation of women's skills. The Ford machinists' case was for the recognition of value of their own skills – women's skills – in their own right.

When the Equal Value Amendment came into force in 1984, as a result of pressure from the European Courts, the machinists' union attempted to steer the case through the extremely complicated and obstructive regulations now in force. Because there was already a job evaluation scheme in existence, the union had to show that it was discriminatory and outdated in order to get a further hearing. They argued that since the scheme had been drawn up in 1967, the EqPA had reformed many social prejudices; that specific comparisons with other jobs clearly showed the scheme to be discriminatory, and that this was inevitable because it had been designed according to a 'felt fair' assessment, by its nature reflective of prejudice; and that the components used for evaluation were given discriminatory weightings.

The Tribunal rejected these arguments.

However, an independent panel convened by the Arbitration, Conciliation and Advisory Service (ACAS) re-evaluated and upgraded the women's jobs according to the original evaluation scheme!

The fragility of the new regulations becomes clear in the light of the Tribunal judgments in the Ford case – particularly in relation to the authority given to antiquated job evaluation methods. However, another recent judgment gives a more optimistic result.

13

Julie Hayward v. *Cammell Laird*. Julie Hayward, who worked as a qualified cook at Cammell Laird Shipyard, claimed equal pay for work of equal value to that of the male joiners, painters, and insulation engineers at the shipyard, in April 1984. There had been no job evaluation at Cammell Laird, and the Tribunal referred the case to an ACAS panel of experts. After 5 months, the report concluded that Ms Hayward's work was of equal value; they measured her job and those of the men against five main areas:

1. Physical demands
2. Environmental demands
3. Planning and decision making
4. Skill and knowledge required
5. Responsibility.

Ms Hayward's victory was the first under the Equal Value Amendment, and resulted in the addition of £30 a week to her pay packet. However, Ms Hayward has yet to see this increase, as a result of a series of appeals by her employers. The amendment has considerable potential for improving the wages of women at work – but the procedures for making a claim are currently too unwieldy and complex to enable women to make full use of them. Without the support of the trade unions, it is unlikely that either Ms Hayward or the Ford machinists would have been able to take their cases as far as they did; and the support of the Trade Unions is not guaranteed, particularly in challenging age-old assumptions about the relative value of men and women's work, and while women are under-represented in the unions.

(b) The Central Arbitration Committee (CAC)

Under the Equal Pay Act, a union can refer to the CAC any pay structure which discriminates against women by providing men-only and women-only rates. Until 1979 the CAC was using its powers fairly widely, but a High Court ruling has since severely restricted its activities. We look at the history of CAC in the field of equal pay, and how its powers should be strengthened on p. 128.

5. Overhauling Opportunity Structures in Employment

As we have mentioned in the section on re-evaluating women's work, such a re-evaluation must be accompanied by a programme to promote the employment of women at all levels in all sectors of work. Such a programme must involve a review of all personnel practices; job descriptions and rates of pay; advertising; interviewing techniques; job specifications; tests; training; perks and provision of facilities; progress assessment and promotion; and redundancy agreements. These practices must be scrutinised by employers and Trade Unions to ensure that any discriminatory elements are eliminated; and positive measures must be taken to counteract the legacy of discrimination against women. We outline a positive action programme in detail on p. 27. If such a programme is accompanied by a fair re-evaluation of the worth of women's jobs, there is a real chance to ensure genuine equality of opportunity for women.

Why do we need Positive Action?

The formal endorsement of the principle of equality for women has certainly helped to change the climate of opinion in the United Kingdom. However, there is considerable evidence to show that it has not substantially altered the position of women in the labour market.

Women still get less pay

In 1975 the average gross hourly earnings of all women workers aged 18 and over, excluding the effect of overtime and shiftwork, were 72.1% of the male equivalent. In 1984, their earnings had increased to 73.5% of men's. The gap between women's and men's weekly pay is even wider, reflecting the longer hours and greater overtime worked by men. So the gap between women's pay and men's pay, after 10 years with the Equal Pay Act, has barely changed.

Women's opportunities are still restricted

The workforce is still conspicuously segregated, with men doing most of the higher paid jobs in higher paid industries and occupations. There are no notable signs that the deeply entrenched prejudices which keep women out of certain jobs have been disturbed by the equality laws. Among professional groups 4% of architects are women, along with 7% of barristers, 22% of doctors, and 8% of scientists, engineers and technologists. Women builders and mechanics are a mere handful. By contrast, women account for 70% of clerks, 77% of workers in catering, cleaning, hairdressing and other personal services, 81% of cleaners and 98% of secretaries and typists. The segregation of women and men into different jobs is not only between industries and occupations, but within them — with women concentrated in the lower-graded, lower-paid jobs. For example, in the Civil Service 76% of the clerical assistants are women, whereas in the higher grades, only 4% of Deputy Secre-

Table 1 Women as a percentage of occupational labour force. Great Britain 1984

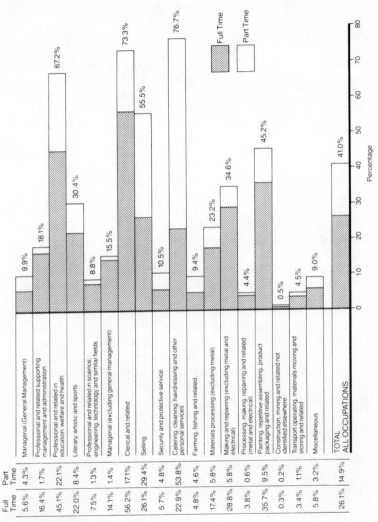

Source: D of E New Earnings Survey 1984.

17

taries are women, and there are no women at all in the top jobs as Permanent Secretaries. Female bar staff earn 13% less than male bar staff; female sales supervisors earn 34% less than males; and female packers earn 24% less than males. Women are trapped in the lower grades by their sex: decisions about promotion are made largely by male managers, most of whom have stereotyped views about what women can or should do at work, and in general it is male employees who are given the chance to train, develop their skills and move into more interesting, better-paid jobs.

Women's paid work, then, is most accurately characterised as poorly-paid, low status, and with very restricted opportunities for advancement. This restriction is a result of systemic discrimination. This often takes the form of direct discrimination — the refusal by both employers and male workers to contemplate the entry of women into non-traditional areas, or the assertion that it is unacceptable to put women in positions of authority over men, for example. Direct discrimination is not necessarily open or expressed; sexual and racial prejudices are often masked by 'rational' argument.

Indirect discrimination is an equally pervasive curtailment of women's job opportunities, and is often a greater barrier to equality because it is subtler and hence harder to challenge head-on. Indirect discrimination takes many forms: in general, however, employment policies and practices are modelled on the characteristics, aspirations and qualifications of the traditional job holder; and given the advantaged position currently occupied by white men in the workforce, the vast majority of better-paid jobs with better prospects are thus indirectly earmarked for them. Men differ from women in that they have in general been able to offer continuous, full-time employability; mobility; different educational backgrounds and qualifications; different work experience; and physical attributes such as brute strength. Employers have demanded such attributes of their prospective employees without examining whether they are really necessary, and thus have discriminated indirectly against women. Under scrutiny, it becomes clear that many requirements imposed both by employers and training agencies do not tally with the real requirements of the job or course. An example of this was shown by Helen Sanders' experience of trying to get training as a carpenter/joiner:

Sanders v. *Manpower Services Commission.* In 1979 Helen Sanders started a TOPS (Training Opportunities) course in carpentry and joinery, at the MSC-run Skillcentre in Leeds. TOPS courses were designed to train people with no previous experience in skilled trades; on Ms. Sanders' course, trainees had to go through a three-week trial period during which their 'trainability' was assessed.

The carpentry and joinery instructor rapidly decided that Ms. Sanders, the only woman on the course, was completely untrainable, and terminated her training. She contested her dismissal at an Industrial Tribunal, under the Sex Discrimination Act: she argued that the tests used to measure 'trainability' were irrelevant and discriminatory. She particularly referred to a strength test which she had been required to pass. This consisted of screwing a 3-inch screw into a piece of wood without first making a pilot hole. *None of the men on the course had been required to do the test*, and furthermore, it involved an exercise which working carpenters do not have to perform. Ms. Sanders had, in fact, passed the test, but considered that it revealed discriminatory attitudes and intentions on the part of the Skillcentre. The Industrial Tribunal did not accept this argument and Ms. Sanders lost her case. The Tribunal thus officially confirmed the Skillcentre's assessment that she was untrainable. However, Ms. Sanders secured a place on an identical course at Wakefield Skillcentre; she completed this course successfully, gained a distinction in the Advanced City and Guilds craft exam, and was later awarded a trophy by Leeds College of Building as their most outstanding student in 1985. She then started teaching carpentry skills. Evidently the methods of assessment used to show that she was untrainable were inadequate and inappropriate.

When the Engineering Industry Training Board decided to establish an experimental programme to train young women to be engineering technicians, it found that its traditional criteria for assessing the quality of its applicants (usually young men) were unconsciously indirectly discriminatory. For example, the EITB's traditional tests of motivation and suitability, which asked about engineering-related hobbies, previous relevant study, and experience, excluded most women who were trying to enter a non-traditional area; yet the women applying for training places were particularly highly-motivated, with the persistence necessary to challenge conformist career expectations. Thames TV, prior to its equal opportunities policy, found its job requirements for camera operators were indirectly discriminatory because if required 'O' level physics which was not a job-related requirement.

In many companies, supervisory and middle management posts are filled by workers from craft and technical sections, which are predominantly or exclusively male, and not from the clerical or administrative sections which include women. An analysis of the job descriptions for such posts often reveals that these criteria are inappropriate. Similarly, great weight is often attached to long periods of shopfloor experience when supervisory and senior posts are to be filled: such criteria can unreasonably discriminate against women, who are likely to spend some time out of the paid workforce looking after children.

Childcare

Indeed, the issue of childcare is crucial to an understanding of women's position in the workforce. Employers frequently argue that efforts to train or promote women will be wasted because women will then leave work to bring up children. In fact the average length of time women leave the paid workforce to care for children is only seven years. Table 2 below shows that the majority of women return to the workforce after having children.

Table 2   Economic activity by age, sex and (for females) marital status
Persons aged 16 and over   Great Britain: Spring 1984

Age	Male	Female	Married female	Other female†
	Economic activity rate* Per cent	Economic activity rate* Per cent	Economic activity rate* Per cent	Economic activity rate* Per cent
16–19	71.2	65.8	42.5	67.2
20–24	90.0	70.4	58.9	80.0
25–34	95.7	60.2	56.2	75.7
35–49	95.9	70.8	70.1	75.5
50–59	87.3	58.7	58.0	61.4
60–64	56.7	21.3	22.0	19.6
65 and over	8.4	3.1	3.7	2.8

† Widowed, divorced, legally separated or single.
§ For definition, see Table 1 and text.
* Economic activity rates are calculated as the numbers economically active as a percentage of the population in the relevant sex and age group.

However, the 'career break' usually results in women having to accept more junior positions on their return to work; and employers' attitudes and the lack of childcare facilities combine to force them into part-time work and deprive them of training opportunities. In 1984, 55% of married women in employment worked part-time, as compared with 23% of non-married women and 4% of men. Childcare facilities are not treated as a priority by employers or training agencies; indeed the MSC has refused either to pay childcare allowances to trainees or to enable them to claim them from the DHSS, on the basis that employers do not make such provision, and that MSC training courses should replicate the conditions of the workplace. Governments, also, do not want to pay for childcare, and in 1984 the UK government even went so far as to implement tax regulations so that for the first time any provision for childcare made by employers would be treated as a perk, and would be taxable on the employee. Thus there is active discouragement of women with children who wish to participate in the labour force on an equal basis. A further example of this is the progressive curtailment of the maternity rights which were established by the Employment Protection Act — to maternity pay, to protection from dismissal, and to reinstatement after childbirth. In 1975, when the Act was passed, a woman who was sacked because of her pregnancy could claim unfair dismissal if she had worked for the same employer for 6 months. In 1979 this qualifying period was extended to one year, and in 1985 it was further lengthened to two years.

Part-time work

Part-time work brings with it many problems in addition to the lower wages. Women do not work in order to pay for luxuries, but in order to support themselves and their dependents. A 1980 Government Central Policy Review showed that without women's earnings, the number of households qualifying for state benefits would increase fourfold. A Department of Employment survey the same year found that a third of women workers worked primarily in order to pay for basic essentials – food and housing. Additionally, almost a fifth of families are headed by a single parent, of whom more than 90% are women. The hopeless inadequacy of childcare provision effectively excludes women with young children from seeking full-time employment.

Thus employers have been able to take their pick of women who are queueing up, desperate for part-time work and in no position to be choosy about wages or working conditions. Nine out of every ten part-timers are women and 80% of these women are employed in the service sector, usually in low-paid jobs such as cleaning, hairdressing, catering and nursing.

Part-time workers, however, are not covered by much of the protective legislation which applies to full-timers. For example, part-time workers cannot claim the maternity rights set out in the Employment Protection Act as mentioned above, unless they work more than 16 hours a week, or have worked more than 8 hours a week for at least 5 years. In theory the protection afforded by the Equality Legislation covers part-time and full-time workers, but in practice part-time workers have been unable to take full advantage of the law, because Industrial Tribunals have held that their work is 'materially different' from that of full-timers.

Similarly, part-timers are largely excluded from pension schemes, holiday agreements, sick pay schemes, and opportunities for training and promotion; and are often discriminated against in union/management agreements on redundancy.

Until the Employment Protection Act is improved to cover all workers, the only way round the problem is for women to job-share, rather than work part-time. This is explained on p. 56.

Homeworkers

Homeworking is another area where women predominate, and where statutory protection is minimal. Homeworking – working for an outside employer in the home– covers such industries as clothing and toy-making, packing and assembly, and, increasingly, new technology. A 1979 survey by the Low Pay Unit (*The Hidden Army* by Simon Crine) showed that most women choose home-working because the constraints of children, disability or local un-employment provide them with little alternative. Wages are meagre, and mostly on a piece-rate basis, and the costs of overheads such as electric power, postage and fares have all to be met by the worker. This set-up is additionally attractive to employers because they have no responsibility for health and safety, or tax and insur-ance, and can lay off the workforce without notice. Because homeworkers are technically self-employed they derive none of the benefits of working for employers; neither do they have the advantage of independence. Lack of trade union organisation leads to isolation and vulnerability.

The effects of recession

Recession and rising unemployment have hit women hard. More women are employed or actively seeking employment than ever before; and to some extent women have been cushioned against job loss as a result of their concentration in the lower-paid service industries, which are expanding. But high unemployment has been used by governments as an excuse for relaxing employment protec-tion laws, thus making life easier for enterprising — or exploitative — employers. The Department of Employment's response to a 1983 European Court of Justice ruling that the UK government was in breach of European Community law by, amongst other things, exempting employers with fewer than six employees from the sex equality laws, was to say that they would attempt to get the Directive amended, because 'it is a major aim of the Government to minimise the burdens imposed by legislation on employers: small enterprises are playing an ever greater part in job and wealth creation and it is particularly important that they should be able to grow and prosper without being hampered by the need to inform themselves about, and comply with, inappropriate restrictions' (*Lifting the Burden*, 1985 White Paper). In this context equal opportunities are deemed very low priority, both by governments and management and, unfortunately, by many Trade Unions.

Along with the repeated extension of the qualifying period for rights under the Employment Protection Act, recent years have seen the semi-privatisation of MSC Skillcentres, which are a major point of access to training for unemployed and unqualified women; and the restriction of the powers of Wages Councils to protect wage levels of the low paid. Four out of five workers covered by Wages Councils are women, a sizeable number of these are Black women; and over the 10 years to 1984, earnings in the Wage Council sector have dropped 8% in relation to the national average, and are now 35% below it. The proposed abolition of wage councils —which are the UK's means of maintaining a minimum wage level — will remove protection altogether from many low-paid non-unionised women workers, in particular migrant workers.

When unemployment is high it also becomes much more difficult for women to break into non-traditional areas of work; and the precept that women should make way for men in the jobs market increasingly informs public and private policy. In reality the effect of this policy is that women have to accept lower wages and worse conditions in order to hang onto the jobs that they — and their dependants — need; and when new jobs are created men are considered the priority.

Education

One reason why women are concentrated in the lower-paid jobs is because our education system does not encourage young women to equip themselves with skills which are saleable on the labour market. Young women are taught that their main responsibilities will be as wives and mothers, which, of necessity, will limit their employability and aspirations. This illusory idea that most women will not need to work is still widespread amongst employers, educators — and young women themselves.

We do not intend here to embark on a detailed analysis of sex-role conditioning. Table 3, however, showing the percentage of female 'O' and 'A' level exam entrants in 1984 in Inner London, demonstrates that even where the education authority (in this case ILEA) has an equal opportunities policy, sex segregation is well underway by the time young people enter the job market.

Table 3 Entries for 'O' and 'A' Level Exams, Summer 1984 (Inner London)

| Subject | % female entrants | | 'A' level |
	CSE 'O' level	GCE 'O' level	
Art	45.8	56.7	65.1
Biology	70.4	60.6	59.2
Craft, Design, Technology	10.9	15.6	6.8
Chemistry	48.7	43.3	41.1
English	51.3	56.0	71.6
French	66.8	62.5	80.3
Geography	46.4	48.0	47.9
History	51.4	50.4	59.4
Home Economics	89.5	94.1	100.0
Mathematics	56.7	43.3	32.3
Physics	24.6	30.8	25.0
Religious Studies	60.4	58.4	72.4
Social Studies	64.9	66.3	76.6

Access to Training

Although women have always gone to work, access to training in skilled trades has been largely restricted to men. Within the workplace, even in predominantly female industries, women are less likely than men to get training – and therefore promotion. For example, only 9% of nurses are men: but they have 45% of the top nursing jobs. Black women are over-represented in the lowest paid work areas, such as cleaning, catering and hospital ancillary work; and women are trapped in these lower grades because their jobs are not considered good training or experience for more senior jobs. Often women do not even get access to information about training and job openings: advertisements, for example, are placed only in publications with primarily male readerships; or careers representatives from local firms visit only the boys' schools. When women do try to break into male-dominated jobs, they run up against considerable hostility from men, which can take the form of sexual harassment and assault.

For example, the London Fire Brigade introduced an Equal Opportunity policy in 1981, and in 1982 the first woman firefighter entered the Service. By 1985 there were 12 women firefighters in London. But within a very short space of time women in the Brigade were making serious allegations of sexual harassment and assault by their male workmates; and although the Brigade had been working on a procedure for dealing with possible complaints of that sort, they were not prepared to deal with them when they arose.

New Technology

Large numbers of women work as unskilled operators in the engineering industries, but only a handful of professional engineers, craftspeople and technologists are women. The development of 'new' technology — electronic engineering and computing — was hailed as the beginning of the end of job segregation in the industry, because it was going to take the dirt out of technology. However, as the new technologies expanded it became apparent not only that it wasn't dirt that was keeping women out of engineering crafts, but also that developments in technology were displacing or de-skilling women operators. Until women are involved in designing, building and maintaining machinery, instead of merely operating it, advances in technology will not improve their working lives.

Low Unionisation

Women are under-represented in Trade Unions, both as members and as paid officials. This is discussed more fully in the section on Unions, p. 83. Equal opportunities have never been a collective bargaining priority for Trades Unions, who have focused instead on working conditions and pay — and on pay, particularly, in terms of the white, male 'family wage-earner'. Trade Unions are the natural vehicle for putting pressure on employers, but until women are more influential in them as both officers and members, the needs of women workers will not be prioritised.

Women are severely disadvantaged in the labour market; and this has been recognised by legislators in the positive action provisions of the SDA. Merely empowering employers to take positive measures is not, however, a particularly effective method of tackling this disadvantage, nor indeed of ensuring that the law is enforced. Many employers are unenthusiastic about the actual requirements of the legislation; and as we have pointed out, there is little sign that they are responding to its non-compulsory provisions for taking positive action. It is clear that a law which merely prohibits discrimination will not change the patterns or effects of past discrimination.

Nonetheless there are notable exceptions to this rule, and in the next section we describe some of the initiatives that have been taken to combat inequality in the workplace.

26

A Programme for Positive Action in Employment

These guidelines for positive action in employment are designed as a basis for negotiations between management and Trade Unions or other workers' groups (e.g. women's committees). We are working on the assumption that both the employer and the workers' group are already committed to agreeing strategies for positive action: the section on Trade Unions deals with how such a commitment might be agitated for.

The guidelines are also aimed at officers who are responsible for developing equal opportunity policies in the workplace, to assist them in devising the most appropriate action for their organisation and in planning priorities.

We are primarily concerned with a revision of the *formal* policies and procedures adopted by different organisations. Although we recognise that any effective positive action policy will also have to challenge the effects of informal networks and agreements, which can have a profound impact on such things as promotion, entitlement to unpaid leave, and access to training, we would in general recommend that *all* personnel procedures and practices should be formalised; and these procedures should be adhered to. All too often, managers resist the introduction of a positive action programme with the argument that it is long-term attitudinal and social change which is needed; and that they cannot take responsibility for this. We accept that attitudes must change, but would argue that change in workplace policies and customs will contribute to wider change. For example, if employers cause managers to change their behaviour, changes in attitudes may result when managers realise that equality of opportunity does not threaten them.

Not all the proposals in this section will be appropriate to every workplace, and some are more easily introduced than others. Very few of them will be expensive. Most will involve simply a review of personnel practices, and taking positive steps to ensure that the preconditions exist for women to take full advantage of the opportunities that exist in the workplace. It is a programme of good employment practices which will enable both women and men to realise their full potential in the workplace.

1. Declare an Equal Opportunity Policy

A number of employers have already declared themselves to be 'Equal Opportunity Employers'. This can mean a great deal, or nothing at all, depending on how strongly the statement is worded, how much support it has within the workforce, and whether and how it is put into practice.

It is important that the policy is discussed and endorsed at all levels of the organisation, by the management as well as by the workers' representatives. The policy must also be widely publicised within the workplace and in all of the company's publicity material — not just in recruitment literature. There are unfortunately many examples of policies which have gone no further than public relations or personnel departments, leaving the people who were supposed to benefit from them in complete ignorance of the new guidelines, and thus unable to take advantage of them.

The TUC has recommended that the following model clause be inserted into a collective agreement wherever unions and management have negotiated an equal opportunities policy:

> The parties to this agreement are committed to the development of positive policies to promote equal opportunity in employment regardless of workers' sex, marital status, creed, colour, race or ethnic origins. This principle will apply in respect of all conditions of work including pay, hours of work, holiday entitlement, overtime and shiftwork, work allocation, guaranteed earnings, sick pay, pensions, recruitment, training, promotion and redundancy.
> The management undertake to draw opportunities for training and promotion to the attention of all eligible employees, and to inform all employees of this agreement on equal opportunity.
> The parties agree that they will review from time to time, through their joint machinery, the operation of this equal opportunity policy.
> If any employee considers that he or she is suffering from unequal treatment on the grounds of sex, marital status, creed, colour, race or ethnic origins he or she may make a complaint which will be dealt with through the agreed procedures for dealing with grievances.

The mention of 'positive policies' in the opening sentence of this clause directly invites management to introduce a positive action policy: certainly this statement in a collective agreement will not in itself be enough to effect change. This may seem an obvious point, but the experience of the past five years has shown that it is common practice for a policy to be negotiated and then for both management and union to leave it at that. A discouraging number of self-styled 'Equal Opportunity Employers' have taken no action whatever to implement their declarations.

Examples of good policies

A good policy is one which makes detailed and specific demands on management, and contains guidelines for enforcement. Thus it can work, it can be seen to work, and it can be assessed and reviewed constantly, to ensure that women are progressing in the organisation. A detailed policy must, however, be preceded by full consultation so that it will be relevant to the needs of the organisation, and will be understood and accepted by the workforce. It must not be so complicated that management claim they cannot enforce it.

Liverpool Health Authority

Liverpool Area Health Authority approved the following equal opportunity policy in 1981, after two years of research and consultation:

Liverpool Area Health Authority (TEACHING)

EMPLOYMENT POLICY

EQUAL OPPORTUNITIES

INTRODUCTION
Equal opportunity can be attained only through an acceptance by the Authority and its employees and their trade unions that the full utilisation of the talents and resources of the entire workforce is important in their own interests and in the interests of the National Health Service as a whole.

An effective equal opportunities policy will enable the Authority to ensure, as far as possible, that there is no unlawful direct or indirect discrimination as well as allowing it to develop good employment practices in respect of all employees.

The Authority's policy aims at positive measures to eliminate not only overt acts of discrimination but also conditions of requirements and practices which are discriminatory in practice.

POLICY STATEMENT

The Liverpool Area Health Authority (Teaching) is an equal opportunity employer. The aim of the Authority's policy is to ensure that no job applicant or employee receives less favourable treatment on the grounds of sex, marital status, age, race, colour, nationality, ethnical or national origins or social background. In addition, such persons will not be disadvantaged by conditions or requirements which cannot be shown to be justified.

Selection criteria and procedures will be frequently reviewed to ensure that individuals are selected, promoted and treated on the basis of their relevant merits and abilities. All employees will be given equal opportunity and, where appropriate, special training to enable them to progress within the National Health Service.

THE RESPONSIBILITY OF THE AUTHORITY

The Authority has a legal obligation to ensure that it and its employees do not discriminate on the grounds of sex, race or social background, etc. The Industrial Code of Practice goes further and states: 'Management should not merely avoid such discrimination, it should develop positive policies to promote equal opportunity in employment'.

Therefore, the responsibility for providing equal opportunity rests primarily with the Authority. This can best be met by an equal opportunity policy which is effectively monitored to ensure that there is no unlawful discrimination and that equal opportunity is genuinely available.

THE RESPONSIBILITIES OF INDIVIDUAL EMPLOYEES

While the overall responsibility for ensuring that there is no unlawful discrimination in an establishment rests mainly with the Authority, individual employees at all levels also have certain responsibilities.

Good employee relations and practices depend on employees perhaps even more than on management and so their attitudes and activities are of crucial importance. They have duties to their employer, to their trade union (where appropriate) and to their fellow employees. In particular individual employees:

1. Should cooperate with measures introduced by management to ensure equal opportunity and non-discrimination.

2. Should not themselves discriminate e.g. as supervisors or management or as persons responsible for selection decisions in recruitment, promotion, transfer, training etc.

3. Should not induce or attempt to induce other employees or unions or management to practice unlawful discrimination.

4. Should not victimise or attempt to victimise individuals on the grounds

that they have made complaints or provided information on discrimination.

5. Should not harass, abuse or intimidate other employees on account of their sex or race, for example in attempts to discourage them from continuing their employment.

6. Should inform management if they suspect that discrimination is taking place in employment decisions.

Managers in particular, should:

1. Make it clear to employees the law and the Authority's policy on equal opportunity.
2. Ensure that grievance are dealt with in a consistent manner.

COMMUNICATIONS

Equal opportunity policies may not by their nature be expected to bring about sudden changes, but persistence, particularly by management and trade unions will in time achieve the objective of realising the full potential of each person in employment to the benefit of the individual, the Authority and the National Health Service in general.

Management should consider the advantage of ensuring that all who have influence over opportunity in the Authority are aware of the policy. It is important that all concerned know clearly what the policy requires of them, in order that they may be encouraged to deal with matters of equal opportunity in a consistent manner.

Full knowledge of the policy will provide a protection against the danger of management accepting discriminatory practices which might otherwise go uncorrected.

The examples set by management and union officials have a very important part to play in breaking down entrenched discriminatory beliefs, and in the morale and aspirations of those who may have been disadvantaged in the past.

Employees should take the initiative by discussing their career prospects and training needs with the appropriate person.

ACTION TO BE TAKEN
1. Review of Policies and Procedures
The Authority will regularly review and, if necessary, revise existing policies and formal and informal procedures to ensure that equal opportunity is available to all employees. In particular, examination will be made to see whether apparently equal policies are producing unequal effects and could be interpreted as being indirectly discriminatory. Where it is found that they are operating or could operate against equal opportunity they will be amended after consultation with Trade Unions where appropriate.

31

2. *Instructions and Pressure to Discriminate*
   Guidance will be issued to all employees, and particularly to Managers, on the law concerning instructions and pressure to discriminate.
   Enquiries will be made into suspected cases of instructions or pressure to discriminate. If direct discrimination is discovered steps will be taken for this to be stopped at once. In such cases disciplinary action may be taken against the individuals concerned. Special guidance and training will also be given to avert future cases of discrimination.

3. *Victimisation*
   Guidance will be given to all employees on the law against victimising individuals who have made complaints of discrimination or provided information about such discrimination.

4. *Review of Policy*
   The Authority will periodically review the arrangements and systems of checking that the policy is being maintained.

MONITORING EQUAL OPPORTUNITY
An effectively monitored equal opportunity policy will enable the Authority to identify groups of employees who are under-represented in certain jobs or sections, to assess the reasons for this, and where appropriate to make use of the Acts' provisions and take positive action.

The information needed for effective monitoring may be obtained in a number of ways but in most cases it will be best provided by means of records. Any such records kept will be solely for the purpose of measuring whether equal opportunity is being afforded.

The policy has several important elements. Whilst placing a great deal of emphasis on the responsibilities of the workforce, it states quite clearly that the Authority will take the major responsibility for equal opportunity. It also stresses the importance of ensuring that all of the Authority's employees know about the policy, not only so that they can abide by it, but also so that they can take advantage of it.

It commits the Authority to providing training in order to avoid discrimination, and to using its powers under the equality legislation to provide training for under-represented groups of the workforce. It also recognises the need for monitoring and reviewing the policy.

This policy has been accompanied by positive measures: monitoring of applications has been undertaken; word-of-mouth recruitment has been banned, and jobs have been advertised more widely. A Race Relations Advisory Committee has been established, and racial discrimination has been identified as an offence in the Authority's disciplinary procedure.

In some respects, however, this policy is still quite hesitant. Although it expresses a commitment to positive action, it gives little detail about precisely how measures will be introduced and monitored. The exception to this is the statement concerning special training, although this has not yet been implemented.

Rank Xerox

An example of a policy which includes detailed proposals as well as clear guidelines for enforcement comes from Rank Xerox. This is an overall policy for Rank Xerox employees around the world, and was first issued in 1976. We quote the section on the employment of women in full; the policy also includes an equally detailed section on racial equality. Whilst not suggesting that this policy is perfect, or has had *any practical effect*, it is obviously the result of careful and thorough research, and provides comprehensive recommendations for action.

1. Employment of Women

The programme is designed to increase the employment of women in all types of job, but especially in Sales, Service, Specialist, Professional and Management posts.

The programme only observes such restraints as are imposed by Law or social pressure and which would make it impossible (not merely unusual or even unique) for a woman to perform a particular job successfully.

1.1. Recruitment of Women

1.1.1. All internal job vacancy forms to be checked to ensure that they make it clear that both men and women are eligible to apply (see 1.1.3 for exceptions).

1.1.2. Each job advertisement (internal and external) to state, in a bold or heavy type, that both men and women are invited to apply (see 1.1.3 for exceptions).

1.1.3. The onus is on the manager raising the staff requisition if the job *must* be reserved for a man, or *must* be reserved for a woman. All managers to be informed of this responsibility and advised that each exception has to be agreed by the Personnel Manager.

1.1.4. Where a female recruiter is employed, and where it is customary for the recruiter's name to be included in the advertisement, she will be properly identified (Miss, Mrs, Ms).

1.1.5. When recruitment visits are made to schools, universities, etc., care is taken to make it clear to the authorities that Rank Xerox is an equal opportunity employer.

1.1.6. Ensure that women's schools, colleges, etc., are specifically included in any recruitment visits.

1.1.7. Ensure that all apprenticeships and initial-entry training schemes are open to both men and women.

1.1.8. Ensure that the Communications (or Public Relations) Department and the Advertising Department and Agency are fully briefed on the policy on employment of women, are given a copy of it and are asked to publicise it as much as possible.

1.1.9. Ensure that all employment agencies working for the company are fully briefed and given a copy of the policy.

1.1.10. Ensure that all recruiting booklets, company booklets, slide lectures, training documents, etc., spell out the policy on employment of women wherever appropriate.

1.2. Management of Women

1.2.1. All managers to be advised that attainment of the objectives of the policy on employment of women is as important as any other traditional business responsibility and that full account of performance will be taken in all future performance reviews.

1.2.2. Revise appraisal documents to include this requirement.

1.2.3. All managers to be briefed on the national legal requirements regarding the employment of women.

1.2.4. Revise managerial job descriptions to include the requirement to develop the employment of women, particularly in Sales, Service, Specialist, Professional and Management posts.

1.3. Promotion of Women

1.3.1. Each senior manager to be advised that he is required to identify a number of suitable developmental posts for women in his area.

1.3.2. Collect responses to 1.3.1., discuss and confirm.

1.3.3. Identify individual women, within the company, who have educational qualifications or high intelligence and the desire to attempt an executive career.

1.3.4. Tailor training and development packages for those identified individuals.

1.3.5. Personnel Manager to review personally the appraisals and development plans for all women above clerical grades, and those within clerical grades identified as having promotion potential.

1.3.6. Wherever a development course is being planned, managers should give full consideration to sending women on the course.

1.4. Pay for Women

1.4.1. All salaries to be checked to ensure that there is equal pay for equal work.

1.4.2. Personnel Manager to check that interpretation of 'equal work' is fair and is not used as a cloak for continued inequality.

1.4.3. Any anomalies to be put right at the next pay review.

1.4.4. Prepare analysis of pay levels and pay awards for all non-clerical female staff.

1.5.1. Collect benchmark data as specified in Equal Opportunity policy document.

1.5.2. Set unit target for increasing employment of women. The target should include annual increases in numbers and percentages of women employed in each of the following categories: Sales, Service, Specialist, Professional, Management and in the total number and percentage of women employed.

1.5.3. Review progress in meeting targets.

A policy of this kind prepares the ground for a real improvement in the position of women and black people, because it gives very clear and exact instructions as to how it should be enforced.

2. Analyse the Workforce

As the objective of an equal opportunity policy is to improve the position of women in all categories and grades within the workforce, it is an essential prerequisite of a positive action programme that a full picture of the workforce is obtained. Thus it will be possible to identify the areas of work, and the grades, at which women are under-represented. It also provides a level against which the future progress of the equal opportunities policy can be measured. Both the EOC and CRE Codes of Practice recommend this analysis.

In order to do an audit of the workforce, take the *categories* of employees in the company or organisation and identify the proportion of men and women in each category. It is essential that the categories used are specific to the company: that they reflect its structure, and that they identify grades (skilled, semi-skilled, technical, clerical, professional) and occupations. Statistics can actually hide job segregation unless they are analysed fully. A 'management' category should thus not include secretarial staff; nor should the predominantly female manual categories — such as cleaning — be indistinguishable from the predominantly male manual categories, such as construction work. The analysis should also identify the position of ethnic minority groups in the workforce — otherwise Black women inevitably become invisible in the statistics — and should include information about the hours people work.

Some employers — notably local authorities — have also collected information about workers' childcare and other dependent care responsibilities. It is important that any information collected on such things is supplied on a voluntary basis; employees should be fully informed as to the purpose of the survey. It is also essential that this information is treated as confidential, and that employees and potential applicants are reassured on this point.

When the categories of employees have been identified, they should be analysed: by salary, 'perks' (such as cars and mortgages), grade, qualifications and years of service. Depending on the degree of sophistication of the personnel records, analyses can be done to compare these factors with each other, breaking them down according to sex. The most obvious point of comparison is the extent to which women and men of the same age with similar qualifications are receiving the same pay.

The statistical analysis is essential in order to gain a detailed picture of the areas of discrimination and disadvantage in the workforce.

Both the Littlewoods Organisation and the Midland Bank have been developing computer systems in order to assist in the collection, monitoring and application of such information; but the analysis does not require any more sophisticated machinery than that which is already used in order to pay wages and National Insurance contributions.

3. Analyse the Organisation

An equal opportunity policy will not work unless it is known about and understood at all levels of the organisation. To be successful, it must become integral to the working of the personnel department. Equal opportunities is an aspect of good management practice, and will not be effective if it is merely the responsibility of one person, who is not centrally placed in the personnel work of the organisation. It is therefore necessary to examine how the organisation functions: what are the lines of responsibility and accountability? How are internal communications organised? For example, if a management policy is changed, will employees be individually informed of this change, or will general notices be posted? Who makes decisions which might affect the implementation of an equal opportunities policy? In order to change the opportunity structure of an organisation it is necessary to know where changes must be agreed: the personnel department may change job requirements without informing the publicity department, thus negating the effects of any new policy.

In some organisations, this kind of analysis will be obvious and straightforward, but in others it will not. For example, in some voluntary organisations (organisations with paid staff members but without statutory funding) equal opportunity policies have been difficult to implement because the procedures for agreeing appointments procedures, the content of advertisements, and job requirements, are informal and unplanned, and there has been resistance to any formalisation of them.

4. Examine Job Definitions and Requirements

The vast majority of jobs are implicitly defined as men's jobs or women's jobs well before the applicants are interviewed. This results partly from the way jobs are described and, more importantly, from the hidden assumptions about the experience and qualifications which the job demands based on who usually does it. A positive action programme requires careful examination of these assumptions and definitions, so that unnecessary requirements can be weeded out. This is particularly important when unemployment levels are high: employers are often overwhelmed by the numbers of job applications they receive, and use arbitrary criteria for pruning them. This frequently takes the form of increasingly stringent and inappropriate requirements which the successful applicants must meet. For example, applicants for manual jobs are asked to produce evidence of academic ability.

Each job should be examined in terms of the real needs of the organisation and the purpose of the job. Job descriptions should reflect these factors, and should be updated if necessary — if a staff member leaves, for example, their job should be reviewed and negotiated with workers' representatives to ensure that the job description is not simply based on a profile of previous jobholders, but reflects the current requirements of the job. It is necessary to determine what requirements are essential, rather than merely traditional, so that people are not unnecessarily excluded from consideration. The following are examples of 'qualifications' which are known to restrict the numbers of women who can apply. Such specifications should be very carefully scrutinised.

(a) Length of experience

Three or four years' experience in a job can be just as valid as twenty years. Women are less likely to have had long years of service in one job because they still have the primary responsibility for childcare and dependent care. The experience which women gain through doing unpaid work — at home, with children, and

37

with community organisations — is largely unrecognised by employers, even though the skills involved in such work are very valuable in the workplace.

(b) Age bars

Imposing minimum age bars for recruits to certain jobs may discriminate against women who have left the labour force temporarily to care for children. For example, the Civil Service Commission used to operate an upper age limit of 28 for applicants to the executive officer grade. Ms. Belinda Price applied for a job and was turned down because she was over 28; she had, like many other women, spent several years in her twenties raising children. She challenged the Civil Service Commission at an Industrial Tribunal on the grounds that the age limit excluded more women than men, and was therefore indirectly discriminatory. The Civil Service argued that they needed the age limit in order to ensure the creation of a 'balanced career structure'; but after a total of three Tribunal hearings they were instructed to raise the age limit, and it is now 45.

(c) Qualifications

Many job advertisements demand certain minimum qualifications, which are frequently irrelevant and unnecessary. Hackney Council Direct Labour Organisation, which is responsible for the Council's building and maintenance work, recently decided to change its recruitment specifications to avoid discrimination. It no longer requires applicants for adult traineeships to have had previous experience, so long as they can show that they are keen to learn a trade. This has resulted in increased applications from women and from Black people. Bradford City Council decided to reduce the amount of information it seeks from job applicants, because as well as being irrelevant, much of it could be used to discriminate.

(d) Physical characteristics

Since the Sex Discrimination Act came into force the Police have changed their policy on height requirements. The London Fire Brigade are considering a similar move: they are also in the process of assessing whether their fitness tests are the best scientific measure of someone's ability to work as a firefighter. One issue they are considering is whether their stipulations about chest size and chest expansion are an accurate determinant of lung capacity.

If a job traditionally has a height or strength requirement, this should be examined. Some requirements actually exceed the limits set by Health and Safety regulations. If a requirement *is* found to be necessary, each individual should be tested separately: men are not invariably stronger than women!

The job should also be examined in terms of any traditional assumptions held by management or employees that the jobholder must be able-bodied. Many employers assume that their staff will all need to be able to see and hear within the normal range, to move about freely, and so on, when in fact the jobs themselves do not require this.

(e) Mobility requirements

Many employers want their staff to be able to move around the country when asked to do so. There may be valid reasons for this requirement, but suiting the employer's convenience is not one of them. It may be necessary for some of the workforce to be mobile in some jobs, but a universal requirement of mobility will inevitably disadvantage women.

Each job should be examined to discover how often employees do actually move, and whether within the group of employees there are enough potentially mobile people to cover the need arising. If mobility is decided on as a selection criterion, care must be taken to ensure that women are not automatically assumed to be non-mobile. Equally, interviewers should not question a candidate's assertion that s/he is mobile. It may be that a female candidate, with or without a family, is able to move; whereas a man cannot do so on account of his wife's job.

Boots and Littlewoods are examples of employers who have re-assessed their mobility requirements and adapted them so as to avoid unfair discrimination. Boots now require branch managers to be mobile only within their region; Littlewoods will consider trainees for promotion even if they are unable to move.

Marks and Spencer, in considering their mobility requirements, have established that the expectation of some senior employees that they will spend nights away from home, and travel a good deal during working hours, has held back women workers. Again, such requirements should be examined very carefully, and abandoned if they are superfluous. The Civil Service has recommended that those designing its training programmes should determine whether residential courses are a necessary part of training; and if they are, whether they can be shortened.

(f) Shift working

Because of the Factories Acts, women are excluded from working certain shifts in many jobs. However, before assuming that women would not be able to do a job because shift work may be occasionally required, it is necessary to consider how often shift work is needed, and whether there are enough men available to cover the need.

All of these are examples of potential forms of indirect discrimination. Unless it can be shown in each and every case that requirements such as those mentioned are essential for the job, they may be proved to be unlawful.

5. Recruitment and Advertising

Employers have encountered great difficulties over the last few years in redesigning their advertising to reflect their equal opportunities policies. This is largely owing to inexperience and lack of relevant knowledge. For example, recruitment officers in the building industry will not have made useful contact with careers teachers in girls' schools. Engineering firms will not have photographs of female apprentices to use in advertising campaigns. Similarly, they will be unaccustomed to advertising in publications which are aimed at young women, or Black people, and they will not know which ones to use. It is important that anyone involved in recruitment for a company is advised of its equal opportunity objectives: even if company personnel have no preconceptions about 'men's work' and 'women's work', the agencies through which they recruit often have.

(a) Recruitment in schools and colleges

It should be made clear to careers advisors in mixed schools and colleges that the company has an equal opportunities policy and is as interested in recruiting young women as young men. Discussion of the equal opportunity policy should form part of any careers talk. Girls' schools should, of course, be included in the round of careers visits; there is some evidence to show that girls are more likely to venture into non-traditional areas of training if they are learning separately from boys. Several local authority Direct Labour Organisations have extended their careers visits to include girls' schools with encouraging results: Hackney DLO has devised an exhibition for these visits, which is specifically designed to interest young women in trades such as plumbing and mechanical engineering.

When a school is visited, it is important that there is not an alternative attraction, which is more likely to appeal to girls at the same time. It is not unusual for schools to arrange careers talks on engineering and nursing simultaneously, which inevitably means that classes are segregated by sex. However, it is helpful on occasion to give talks to girls only, so that they are not inhibited from asking questions and discussing jobs which are not commonly done by women. It also makes a considerable difference if the talk is given by a woman — for example, a woman engineer — as this provides students with convincing evidence that women can get such jobs.

(b) Job centres and employment agencies

It is essential to make it quite explicit to the staff at the local job-centre or employment agency that male and female candidates will be considered for all jobs. Such agencies commonly assume that because a particular company has only hired men for certain jobs in the past, they will only consider men in the future. In 1984 the Women's National Commission, a Government-sponsored body, conducted research into training opportunities for women, and commented that:

> . . . the approach and advice of jobcentre staff can be inimical to women's aspirations for non-traditional training, and sometimes their wish to have any kind of job in competition with men.

Jobcentre employees should be sent a copy of the company's equal opportunity policy, and asked not only to be mindful of it when making referrals, but also to draw it to the attention of all potential job candidates.

Some firms have their own employment agencies. Boots, for example, has a drop-in centre in the middle of Nottingham which provides information about jobs with the firm. Other companies have run mobile exhibitions, which can tour an area with re-cruitment information. These can be a very effective means of targetting groups of potential employees.

(c) Advertising in newspapers and magazines

It is not enough simply to publish advertisements which state that a job is available to men and women, or even that the company is an 'equal opportunity employer' — although this is an important first step. All too often, employers who do this find that women still do not apply for jobs which are traditionally done by men;

they then wrongly conclude that women are simply not interested. It is more likely that women have not seen the advertisements, or have assumed they were not intended for them. To ensure that this does not happen, the wording of the advertisement should stress that female applicants would be welcome. If the advertisement is illustrated, it should show women doing the job. Finally, the advertisement should be placed in magazines which are aimed at women. It is not enough to place advertisements in publications with a mixed readership: women will not look at job vacancies for car mechanics if they appear in the local paper; they will take notice, however, if they see a similar advertisement in a women's magazine.

Advertising campaigns designed along these lines have proved very effective in increasing the numbers of female applicants. It is important that the company's general publicity material also reflects the equal opportunity policy: women will often remember such material when they hear of job vacancies, and may be deterred from applying if it has no equal opportunity content.

(d) Informal recruitment

A lot of jobs are filled via recommendations from current members of the workforce. In some occupations, particularly in certain crafts, recruitment of new workers is almost exclusively from the sons of male workers. Men could be encouraged to recommend female members of their family for employment but this will inevitably result in the perpetuation of racially discriminatory recruitment practices. Jobs should be advertised internally first, so that existing employees have a chance to learn and develop skills within a company; but external advertising should be not confined to a pool of friends and relatives of the existing workforce. Internal applicants will always have the edge over outsiders, but unless outsiders have a chance to apply, the employment profile will remain unchanged.

Recruitment is often initiated at the factory gate, over the telephone, or by receptionists. Staff at this first point of contact should be instructed to be particularly careful not to discourage women from pursuing inquiries; but ideally, all recruitment procedures should be formalised, and all inquiries should be rerouted through the formal application procedure.

(e) Special measures to recruit women

Some employers have put a great deal of effort into rectifying the under-representation of women in their workforce. The London Fire Brigade, for example, has set up an equal opportunities unit with the specific task of ensuring that more women and people from ethnic minority groups join the fire service. They have run special advertising campaigns; have publicised training opportunities more widely than ever before; and have consulted with a range of women's employment projects and groups such as Women And Manual Trades. They have also targetted women in occupations where there is a high level of unemployment and where women might have relevant skills; thus, for example, personnel officers have visited groups of women who are training to be sports teachers or nurses, to tell them about opportunities in the fire service. Some local authorities have used similar 'saturation' techniques, and have ventured into new areas of advertising, such as local radio and television. Although this can be expensive, particularly for employers who have not previously had to make the slightest effort to fill job vacancies, it is a very speedy and effective way of enforcing an equal opportunity policy. As long as the rest of the policy is implemented, such advertising can shortcut more longwinded procedures for redressing imbalances.

However, it is not sufficient for an employer to run specific advertising campaigns for women, without revising the content of the remainder of their publicity material. The Construction Industry Training Board produced a leaflet in 1984 designed to encourage young women to apply for places in Youth Training Schemes in the industry. This showed pictures of women construction workers, alongside enthusiastic assurances that women were needed in the building industries. However, the remainder of the CITB's publicity material does not reflect this initiative in any way: leaflets publicising other training schemes are still illustrated exclusively with pictures of men, and contain no references to opportunities for women.

(f) Keeping within the law

Although the advertising provisions in the SDA and RRA were the most immediately and startlingly effective, the area of advertising has proved an extremely thorny one for equal opportunity employers. Employers have adopted different approaches to publicising their equal opportunity policies. Some, like ICI, British Gas and the Civil Service, merely state at the bottom of advertisements that they are equal opportunity employers. Others, including many community groups, health authorities, and local councils adopt a more explicit wording such as:

> . . . we encourage applicants from all sections of the community, regardless of sex, ethnic origin, race and marital status.

This list may also include such things as culture, sexual orientation or disability.

43

Still others — most notably local authorities — have responded to the positive action sections of the equality legislation with statements such as:

> ... we positively welcome applications from Black people, disabled people and women, where they are under-represented in particular jobs.

Statements such as these have fallen foul of some local and national newspapers, jobcentres, and indeed the Commission for Racial Equality. The objection raised is that such a statement reveals an intention to discriminate at the point of recruitment.

We strongly refute this objection: it is important that equal opportunity employers do not overstep the law, but it is also essential that they are able to publicise their policies effectively, and do so explicitly.

The above statement has not been 'tested' in the courts: but although the legislation prohibits employers from employing selectively in order to counteract the effects of past discrimination, it does *not* prohibit them from advertising selectively, or to obtain a representative group of applicants. So long as employers are clear that such advertising is intended to attract women who will then be judged on an equal basis with male applicants, they have no need to worry about breaking the law.

At the same time other advertisements, whilst not strictly speaking unlawful, certainly fall short of the spirit of the law. One example of this is an advertisement for technicians run by Kodak in 1985, which was headlined:

[Are you] Bright? Well motivated? Man Manager?

Although this wording does not exactly specify that applicants must be male, it certainly implies that the existing workforce is exclusively male. Women are undoubtedly deterred from applying for jobs which are advertised in this way.

A similar practice is that adopted by London Regional Transport: although LRT has an equal opportunity policy they continue to advertise for 'Railmen' on hoardings in tube and bus stations. These advertisements are footnoted 'all jobs are open to both men and women', but there is still an implicit message that women are not expected to apply. Since the enforcement of the SDA, it is no longer acceptable for advertisers to claim that the term 'men' includes — and is universally understood to include — both men and women.

It is therefore essential that employers spell out their intentions to give *equal* consideration to applications from women, in all their advertising.

(g) Monitoring applications

To make sure that their advertising reaches as wide a section of the community as possible, employers should monitor the applications they receive, in the same way as they analyse the existing workforce. The monitoring exercise should include unsuccessful applicants as well as successful ones. Information collected for this purpose should, of course, be *confidential*, and should be kept separate from application forms so that those drawing up shortlists cannot use it to discriminate. The monitoring scheme should be explained to all applicants, and they should be informed of the voluntary and confidential nature of the evidence. The London Borough of Camden uses an application form with a detachable slip, on which applicants give details as to their sex and ethnic origin; Bradford City Council is considering a similar format.

6. Application Forms, Tests and Interviews

The process of selection is of course very important. Unfortunately it is often over-simplified, which makes the process prone to discriminatory bias.

(a) Forms

Job application forms should be examined to ensure that all questions asked are actually necessary. The most obvious pitfall to avoid is asking questions about candidates' domestic responsibilities. It is really no business of a potential employer to know how many children a candidate has, and is only likely to prejudice the minds of some of those responsible for hiring who may feel that women with children shouldn't work, or if they do, will be unreliable because of their domestic responsibilities. Such attitudes give rise to direct discrimination, and in any case, are not justified by evidence of women's reliability as workers. It is also not necessary — or desirable — to ask for details of applicants' marital status or nationality.

One way of convincing female applicants that the equal opportunity policy is sincere is to make it clear in the job specification that a period of time spent out of the labour market bringing up children is not regarded as irrelevant and will be taken into account as a useful experience. All the evidence shows that women returning to work are very reliable, mature and stable workers.

(b) Tests

If jobs tests are used, these should be intended to test the skills and aptitudes that the job actually requires. Employers should carry out studies to establish the accuracy of the tests in relation to the characteristic they are supposed to predict, for example, job performance. No test should be used which has not been 'validated' in this way.

Testers should be aware that there is evidence to indicate that there are sex differences in testing. For example, the *average* performance of men and women differ in tests for speed, co-ordination of big bodily movements, spatial ability, manual dexterity, speed of perception, verbal fluency and memory. Differences also arise from, among other things, socialisation and schooling. However these comments deal only with average performance; there will be considerable overlap in individual performances. For example it is quite possible that a particular woman will perform better in tests for speed, co-ordination, big bodily movements and spatial ability than male applicants, while these skills are supposed to be the ones in which the average male performs better than the average female. This illustrates the importance of testing all applicants and not assuming certain skills and aptitudes on the basis of sex.

However, for many jobs, testing should be totally unnecessary as no specific skills and qualifications are required. Such jobs can be easily learned through training, and a prior testing process would be a waste of time. (See 'Saunders *v*. MSC' p. 18.)

(c) Interviews

Interviewing candidates for jobs, or for internal promotion, is obviously an extremely important moment in the selection process. Research studies have shown that as a method of predicting future performance, interviews are an extremely fallible instrument. Well planned interviews and well trained interviewers can produce very good results. Often, however, interviews can be the moment when unbridled prejudice, albeit unconscious, is allowed to affect the decision.

The point of the interview is to find out more about the candidates than can be gleaned from formal written applications and references. It is the occasion when an attempt is made to judge not only the candidate's actual competence in the skills they claim to have, but also their personality. It is also the occasion when the interviewer can try to assess whether the candidates will 'fit in' or, more simply, whether they like them. Precisely because of the subjective nature of these decisions and the relative intimacy of the interview procedure itself, it is particularly important that every effort is made to systematise the process and prevent irrelevant attitudes and responses affecting decisions.

(i) All those participating in interviews should be trained not only in the techniques and practice of interviews, but also in the legal aspects. Obviously it is a long-term proposition for all personnel officers, line managers and other representatives to be trained. In the meantime, no interview should take place without a trained interviewer present throughout the process and contributing to the final decision.

(ii) Those involved in the interviewing should decide what characteristics are relevant to the job (and what are not relevant) and plan beforehand roughly what questions should be asked to elicit appropriate information from the candidates. In general, questions about a candidate's personal circumstances are not relevant and should be avoided. When a candidate has been offered a job, it may be necessary to know about his or her family or home circumstances because of pension schemes etc., but, except in special circumstances (for instance, when the job is residential or requires a great deal of travelling), prying into people's personal circumstances or asking about their intentions with regard to children is at best impertinent, and at worst offensive. And since such questions are rarely asked of male candidates, it could be assumed by women to show an intention to discriminate against them.

(iii) Where possible, more than one interviewer should be used so that the possible prejudice of a single interviewer need not be a decisive factor.

(iv) Interview boards should include women as well as men, and members of ethnic minority groups as well as white people.

7. Contracts of Employment

Trade Union negotiators and employers frequently overlook contracts of employment when revising policies and procedures. Sometimes this is because the terms of the contract bear little relation to what employees expect or are expected to do, and thus the contract becomes irrelevant to negotiations with management; sometimes it is because the contract contains very little information. And frequently, of course, employees are simply not issued with copies of their terms and conditions of employment.

Every employee has a statutory right under the 1978 Employment Protection (Consolidation) Act to receive a contract of employment. This contract must identify the employer and the employee, and it must specify: the job title and the date at which employment started; the rate of pay; the hours of work; the entitlement to holiday and leave; the length of notice required; and the grievance and disciplinary procedures. Certain of these specifications are subject to minimum legal requirements. The terms and conditions laid out in the contract are a legitimate subject for Trade Union negotiations; it is therefore very important that they are reviewed under any positive action programme, and that the contract is perceived as one of the safeguards protecting such a programme.

Contracts vary enormously from one organisation to another, as does the extent to which they are implemented. However, any agreement between management and the Trade Unions can easily be breached if it is not formalised: thus, as soon as an equal opportunity policy is agreed in an organisation, it should be incorporated into the contract of employment. The following are points which should be given particular attention:

(a) *Enforcing the equal opportunity policy:* the contract should clearly specify the responsibilities of employers to enforce the policy. It should equally clearly specify the duties of employees to adhere to the policy, and any attempt to frustrate the policy (such as racial or sexual harassment) should be construed as a serious disciplinary offence.

(b) *Leave entitlement:* where agreement has been reached on entitlement to parental or responsibility leave, this should be specified. There is otherwise no guarantee that employees will be able to exercise rights which are above the statutory minimum requirements.

(c) *Temporary and short-term contracts:* these are frequently issued by employers who are not sufficiently financially secure to offer long-term employment. Employers should first ensure that the reasons for offering only short-term employment are justified. If they can justify the practice, they should ensure that women workers are not bearing the brunt of their financial instability. They should therefore monitor the issuing of such contracts, and rectify any discriminatory practices. A 1985 survey by the National Union of Teachers found that of all teachers working on fixed-term contracts, 96% of the part-timers and 81% of the full-timers were women.

(d) *Probationary periods:* many contracts of employment specify that the employee has been hired subject to approval after a probationary period. The period specified varies from place to place, and in some cases may be extended. In theory an employer could contrive to extend such a period indefinitely but after a year (or 2 years where there are fewer than 20 employees) an employee would have some rights to equal treatment under the Employment Protection (Consolidation) Act.

In general we would not endorse the use of probationary clauses. Firstly, employers should ensure that their application forms, tests, and interviews provide them with sufficient information to assess a person's suitability to do a job: they should not engage in speculative recruitment. If their methods of recruitment are inadequate they should be changed. Secondly, placing people on probation is a very effective means of ensuring that they do not complain about conditions at work, including discriminatory practices. And thirdly, the use of a probationary period creates a power imbalance between new and old workers. An organisation may start to recruit women for the first time as the result of a positive action programme; and if these women are all on probation they will immediately be placed at a disadvantage in relation to their male co-workers. The same thing will apply if an organisation which has never employed Black people starts to do so as a result of an equal opportunities policy. If organisational conflict then results from the policy, it will be the new workers who are under scrutiny, and are therefore vulnerable. Thus having a probationary period can result in indirect discrimination, as well as being patently unfair; and can obstruct the effective introdution of equal opportunities into the workplace.

If genuine problems arise with new employees, they should be dealt with under the grievance or disciplinary procedure, which should, of course, have a specific equal opportunity content.

We are not suggesting that employers do not need to conduct some form of appraisal of their employees' work, or indeed that employees would not benefit from the opportunity to discuss priorities and job content with management; but such an appraisal should not put people's employment in jeopardy. We discuss the subject of progress appraisal on page 61.

8. Unsuccessful Candidates

Women and men who have failed in their applications for employment, training, transfer or promotion, should be given full details to explain why, so that they have a chance to improve in subsequent applications. Furnishing an explanation will also help them to establish whether or not they have been subject to unlawful sex or race discrimination.

Employers should also consider adopting an appeals procedure for unsuccessful applicants. Nottingham City Council has a detailed recruitment appeals procedure, whereby applicants who consider that they have been discriminated against on the grounds of race, sex, disability, sexual orientation, or spent criminal records, can appeal against the decision. The appeal then freezes any appointment connected with the post, unless a contract has been signed, and the appeal is conducted formally in the presence of equal opportunities personnel. Applicants also have the chance to be represented by, for example, Trade Union officers. If an appeal is upheld, the applicant may be financially compensated or offered another job with the Council.

9. Provision for Employees with Parental Responsibilities

The responsibility for childcare and care of other dependents still remains primarily in the hands of women, and employers should take account of this when they set out to encourage women to apply for jobs on equal terms with men. Inadequate childcare provision is one of the greatest obstacles to women's equal participation in the workforce, and management should tackle the issue as a major priority.

(a) *Maternity and Paternity leave* (taken for the birth of a child). Generous maternity leave is an essential part of any positive action programme.

Contractual arrangements for leave should not be confined to maternity leave (see Contracts, p. 48) but should include a paternity leave option as well as provisions for adoption leave, and leave for employees who have a primary support role in caring for new-born children. Such recognition as there is of workers' childcare responsibilities is still based, in law, on an increasingly outdated, heterosexual, and culturally-biased model of nuclear family life: it does not acknowledge the needs of single parents, nor does it encompass changing lifestyles and patterns of childcare. Provision should cover adoptive parents, and employers who are committed to shared childcare arrangements.

Many employers are now recognising the inadequacies of the statutory maternity leave provision, and are taking appropriate steps. These include extending the allowed periods of paid and unpaid leave; enabling employees on leave to accrue holiday entitlement or retain the use of company cars; and continuing with superannuation payments.

(b) *Parental leave*. It is important for employers to recognise that male workers as well as female workers have parental responsibilities. In 1983, the European Commission published a draft Directive on Parental Leave, which would allow one or other parent to take a minimum of 3 months' leave from work to care for a child under 2 (or under 5 for a child with disabilities). The Directive has not yet been passed by the European Council of Ministers, as a result of the UK Government's veto.

(c) *Responsibility leave*. A certain number of days' annual leave, on full pay and in addition to holiday entitlement, should be made available to female and male employees who need to care for sick children and other dependents.

Smiths' Industries allows employees to take time off for 'non-personal' sickness, depending on their status, length of service, and employment record; and also depending on the closeness of the family relationship. The London Borough of Lewisham has a detailed policy on dependants' leave, which also specifies such conditions for leave entitlement, but acknowledges non-familial relationships (and hence lesbian and gay relationships and relationships between adults and children who live in the same household). This policy, however, differentiates between manual and non-manual workers.

(d) *Flexible hours*. For many women the major difficulties with childcare arise when their children start school. Employees should have the option of working flexitime, with core hours which are within the school day, so that they can meet their domestic responsibilities. Both men and women should also have the option of working part-time, in all spheres of work. For many women, the chance to work flexible hours can be the crucial factor enabling them to work at all.

(e) *Re-entry and reservist schemes*. Women should not be placed at a disadvantage if they leave the workforce temporarily to care for children. Some employers, such as NatWest Bank, have now adopted schemes whereby women who leave work for family reasons can return to similar jobs up to five years later. Re-entry schemes should also be available to men: otherwise they may be unlawful. Boots has recently introduced such a scheme in its Retail Division: women exercising this option receive regular bulletins from the company, and are required to 'reserve' their places by working there for a few weeks of each year's absence from full employment. However, the women who can take advantage of this are selected by management at Boots; and, as with most employers who have introduced a re-entry scheme, it is restricted to women at middle-management level and above. A positive action programme should encompass the needs of all women at work, not merely those who have reached higher grades; and there are considerable advantages to employers in encouraging the 'company loyalty' that is fostered by reserving jobs for women who leave work to have children. Such loyalty from staff members at all grades can greatly simplify the job of management!

(f) *Childcare provision.* Employers should seriously consider whether they can provide any nursery or other childcare facilities for their staff. They are often daunted by the supposedly prohibitive costs of such provision, but it can prove an extremely cost-effective measure, in terms of reducing staff turnover and absenteeism. Liverpool Health Authority provides accommodation for a self-financing creche, which is funded by charges to parents on a sliding scale. The Civil Service, also, is starting to provide initial administrative and financial support to daycare schemes which will eventually become self-supporting. Employers should not overlook the need for additional provision during school holidays. For instance, staff with responsibility for school-age children should be given priority when dates for staff holidays are being fixed, so that they can take leave when schools are on holiday. Some employers also enable staff to take unpaid leave during school holidays.

It is every bit as important that training agencies make provision for childcare. The major government training body, the Manpower Services Commission, has repeatedly refused to consider any provision on the basis that their training should 'replicate the conditions of the workplace'. Some local authorities and women's employment projects have responded to the obvious demand for training places with nursery provision or childcare allowances by setting up women's training schemes, which make this provision. There are still only a handful of these women's training workshops, however, and they are invariably over-subscribed.

10. Employees with Disabilities

As well as fulfilling their responsibilities under the Disabled Persons' Acts, employers should ensure that they make appropriate provision for employees with disabilities. For example, if a company is moving premises, or expanding existing premises, reasonable access to the building, and within it, should be a major priority.

Buildings should be easily reached by public transport and should be properly lighted, both inside and outside. This is important not just in terms of disabled access; any organisation that employs women should ensure that the workplace is safe, and that staff leaving work do not have to wait in, or walk through, dark and isolated areas.

Making a building internally accessible involves ensuring that corridors and doorways are wide enough to take wheelchairs; that seating, work surfaces and equipment can be adapted for use by people with disabilities; and that there are lifts and adapted toilets. Most existing buildings are totally inadequate, even in terms of basic health and safety requirements such as adequate lighting and fire protection. Employers should ensure that *all* their staff have a safe working environment. Doors can often be widened, bars fitted in toilets, and ramps installed, at minimal cost. Similarly, whenever new equipment is purchased employers can ensure that it is appropriate to the needs of all existing *and potential* employees.

11. Policies to Combat Sexual and Racial Harassment

Sexual and racial harassment result from sexist and racist attitudes and are a major source of stress for women at work. Employers have a legal obligation to provide a stress-free working environment, and to prevent discriminatory practices and actions on the part of their staff. They should therefore take all complaints of harassment seriously, and deal with them swiftly and sympathetically. Where a complaint proves well-founded, appropriate disciplinary action should be taken.

It is in their interest to deal with harassment before it becomes a source of disruption and friction at work, as it results in sickness, poor working relationships, low productivity and the loss of experienced staff.

Employers should adopt separate definitions for sexual harassment and racial harassment, and should institute and enforce policies and procedures to deal with, and prevent, acts of harassment. Managers and supervisors should be trained in the implementation of the company's equal opportunity policy, and particularly how to deal with complaints of harassment. Employees should be trained to understand the individual's responsibility for ensuring that harassment becomes unacceptable behaviour in the workplace.

Sexual Harassment

We recommend the following guidelines for a policy and procedure on sexual harassment:

Definition

Sexual harassment involves attentions of a sexual nature which are *unwanted* and *unreciprocated*. It might create a stressful or intimidating work environment or threaten a woman's job security. It can range from repeated comments, looks, jokes, suggestions and touching, to sexual assault. It may also include the defacement of personal property; writing graffiti; and circulating or displaying sexually explicit material, or material which makes sexual references to individuals at work.

One of the difficulties in reaching a definition of sexual harassment is that it is necessarily subjective. Ambiguous sexual remarks or suggestions would have to be repeated before they are established as harassment. However, repetition is not always necessary to bring behaviour into the definition of sexual harassment: putting up pin-ups or assaulting a workmate would only have to occur once for the disciplinary procedure to be invoked.

Policy and Procedure

1. Sexual harassment of an employee by any other employee will not be tolerated and is contrary to the employer's policy.
2. It shall be a violation of this policy for any employee with the authority to take or influence personnel actions to:
   - make sexual advances, demands or suggestions to employees over whom that person has authority;
   - grant, recommend, or refuse to take a personnel action based on sexual demands;
   - take or fail to take a personnel action as a reprisal against an employee for rejecting such demands or reporting sexual harassment.
3. The employer will take prompt, corrective action upon becoming aware that incidents involving sexual harassment have taken place.
4. Sexual harassment will be grounds for disciplinary action.
5. Supervisors have an affirmative duty to maintain their workplace free from sexual harassment and intimidation.
6. Employees subjected to sexual harassment should report such conduct to a specified management figure.
7. Supervisors should immediately report to a specified person any complaints of sexual harassment.

54

8. The employer's policy and the procedures to be followed will be communicated to employees as part of training and induction programmes.

Racial Harassment

Definition

Racial harassment involves any expression of racial hatred: repeated verbal abuse, including 'jokes' about supposed racial or cultural characteristics; written abuse; discriminatory treatment of people on racial grounds; the enforced segregation or isolation of one's workmates on the basis of racial difference; physical assault; and threatening behaviour. It may be carried out by individuals or by groups of people; it also includes the incitement of others to the expression of racial hatred, and the publication and circulation of racist material.

Policy and Procedure

1. Racial harassment of an employee by any other employee will not be tolerated and is contrary to the employer's policy.
2. It shall be a violation of this policy for any employee with the authority to take or influence personnel actions to:
   - use any expression of racial hatred to employees over whom that person has authority;
   - grant, recommend, or refuse to take a personnel action based on racial prejudice;
   - take or fail to take personnel action as a reprisal against an employee who has made a complaint of racial harassment.
3. The employer will take prompt, corrective action upon becoming aware that incidents involving racial harassment have taken place.
4. Racial harassment will be grounds for disciplinary action.
5. Supervisors have an affirmative duty to maintain their workplace free from racial harassment and intimidation.
6. Employees subject to racial harassment should report such conduct to a specified management figure.
7. Supervisors should immediately report to a specified person any complaints of racial harassment.
8. The employer's policy and the procedures to be followed will be communicated to employees as part of training and induction programmes.

12. Part-time Workers and Job-sharing

Although the law does not afford part-time workers the same employment rights as full-time workers, there is nothing to stop employers from extending equal rights to all their part-time staff. As long as the vast majority of part-time workers are women, unequal rights for part-timers amount to discrimination against women. A positive action programme should include an agreement that part-timers therefore enjoy full protection against redundancy, right to reinstatement after parental leave, equal pay pro rata, equal job, promotion and training opportunities, and equal access to all positive action measures.

Employers may also consider introducing a job-sharing scheme as an alternative to employing part-timers. This would enable employees to work more flexible hours, is also a way of improving the quality and availability of part-time work, and means that valuable training is not wasted if a skilled person opts to work fewer hours because of childcare responsibilities.

Job-sharing involves employing two people to share one full-time job. Each sharer does half the work and receives half the pay, holiday and other entitlements of the job; and they have the same rights to promotion and employment protection as full-time workers. Almost any job can be shared: schemes have been introduced for people working as teachers, assembly workers, doctors, training managers, clerical staff, and construction workers. Job-sharing involves minimal additional costs to employers; and apart from giving women an additional incentive to continue to work after having children, thus reducing staff turnover and training costs, it also enables employers greater flexibility. For instance, additional cover is available for busy periods, and there is greater continuity when staff changes occur. The Confederation of British Industry noted in 1981 that 'those companies who are experimenting with job-sharing are finding it can lead to increased productivity, lower turnover and reduced absenteeism'.

The Government has introduced incentives for employers to run job-splitting schemes — which are very different from job-sharing schemes. Job-splitting involves splitting jobs in half to make two part-time jobs, and is aimed mainly at low-paid jobs, and at unemployed people who receive state benefits. This discriminates against married women, who do not receive benefit in their own names; and people working in job-splits do not of course, have the same rights as full-time workers or job-sharers.

13. Training

Job-related training

This can have two functions. Firstly it can develop individual expertise in the job and in the work of the organisation; and secondly, it can be part of a programme of staff development enabling individuals to acquire new, transferable skills, in preparation for jobs they do not yet hold.

The former function is fairly widely available in employment and might take the form of an induction programme, day release and short courses etc. The secretary might be trained to use the word processor, the personnel manager in responsibility under the legislation relating to employment and the shopfloor worker in how to use a new machine. The latter function, however, is only available to a few as part of an identifiable career progression within the organisation. Thus the young graduate recruited to a personnel department might get time off work to prepare for personnel management examinations while a shopfloor supervisor probably would not.

The way that training opportunities tend to be linked to career paths and certain types of jobs, in the context of job segregation means that women have access to fewer training programmes and those that are available are more limited, concerned with a particular job rather than opening up new ones.

As part of an equal opportunity policy an employer should:

(a) in the first place: commit itself to providing its staff with training opportunities, so that they can improve job opportunities and acquire transferable skills;
(b) review expenditure for training and development on different categories of staff, paying particular attention to categories that are predominantly female or male to ensure that unjustified priority is not given to male categories;
(c) review recruitment procedures for training opportunities to ensure that they are open to, and encourage applications from, both women and men. Qualifications and experience requirements can disadvantage women and should be avoided unless essential;
(d) ensure that all training opportunities are open to part-time workers: this is particularly important for those designed to facilitate career progression, as 40% of women workers are part-time;
(e) ensure that access to training opportunity is not inhibited as a

57

consequence of family responsibilities. For example, women with children can find it difficult to take part in residential courses;

(f) ensure that the training available is appropriate to the needs of the workforce. This involves regular revision of the nature and content of training courses, to make sure that they continue to provide training in relevant, saleable skills;

(g) ensure that improved or new training opportunities provided for women are reflected in the promotion policies of the company. This means, of course, that the benefits of improved training are fully utilised by the employer.

Training opportunities in the GLC

In 1985 the Greater London Council conducted research into career development opportunities for staff working as data preparation officers in their Central Computer Service, and as typists and word processors in their Central Reprographic Service. The research examined existing opportunities for training; working conditions; staff isolation; discrimination; health factors; job dissatisfaction; barriers to training; and staff interest in training. Women working in the Computer and Reprographic Services were found to be disadvantaged in several ways, and, in particular, the lack of training and career development opportunities prevented women from developing their skills and hence their careers. Women also expressed interest in learning new skills, to enable them to change their jobs within the GLC completely: for instance, women in the Reprographic Service wanted to learn computing skills, and vice versa.

A list of recommendations was drawn up on the basis of the research findings and some action resulted. The GLC Equal Opportunities Group developed a day-release 'Open Options' course, with Southwark College, to teach women office skills, career planning and new technology training. Forty-three staff members had enrolled for this course by May 1985; internal courses were also set up in career development; assertiveness skills; first steps to management; group skills; and personal effectiveness in interviewing. Clerical secondments were also set up for women in the Computer Service, as were supervisory and technical training courses.

Monitoring of training

The monitoring of the take up rate of training opportunities and their effect enables the continual revision of the training policy in response to identified need and areas of risk. In particular, organisations should:

(a) Monitor training programmes with particular reference to the failure of women to take up available opportunities.
(b) Maintain records of training effort and expenditure for male and female employees.
(c) Follow the career progress of those involved. Detailed investigation of training opportunities may reveal the need for women-only courses. Such courses can be specially designed to incorporate the previous experience of the women which, in non-traditional areas of employment, may be limited. Experience has shown that women often do better in single sex groups as past discrimination and disadvantage has taught women to undervalue their skills and experience. Lack of confidence, combined with lack of practice, can limit the progress of women in mixed groups.

Equal Opportunities training

Training has an important part to play in breaking down the discrimination which has led to job segregation. Equal opportunities training involves training for all employees, to help them challenge the stereotyping which reinforces job-segregation.

As part of a positive policy towards equal opportunities, an organisation should:

(a) Develop training programmes designed to compensate women for past discrimination and disadvantage.
(b) Develop a training policy designed to give employees the skills to operate the equal opportunity policy. There are three areas of practice which need special attention:
    i. interviewing job applicants;
    ii. referral of job applicants and employees seeking promotion or transfer, and subsequent selection;
    iii. appraisal of individual progress.

Employees concerned with any of these areas should be trained in their responsibilities under the policy. It is also vital to explain the policy to all employees. Courses, seminars and discussion groups can play a part in this.

14. Redundancy Agreements

It is a fairly common practice in the UK for part-time workers to be the first victims of redundancy schemes to operate on a 'last in, first out' basis. Employers and Trade Union negotiators should give careful consideration to how this affects their equal opportunities policies. For example, the following points should be included in a positive action programme:

(a) Equal protection for part-time workers
(b) No loss of seniority for employees returning from parental leave
(c) If redundancies are unavoidable, they should be spread across female and male jobs.

15. Pension Schemes

The Equality Legislation does not cover state benefits, including pensions; and state-operated workplace pension schemes are earnings-related, so that higher earners receive bigger pensions.

Where organisations run their own pension schemes, they should ensure that women have equal access to them: lower age limits on entry, for example, should not exclude more women than men; part-timers should not be excluded; women should be permitted to transfer their pension rights to their husbands in case of their death; and staff should not lose pension rights through taking parental leave.

Under current legislation the retirement age for women is 60, and for men 65. This inequality disadvantages both men who wish to retire early, and women who wish to continue working. After the age of 60, women have no right to redundancy pay. However, employers can contract to employ people past retirement age, and an organisation operating a positive action programme should guarantee female and male employees equal rights to redundancy payments at all ages. As of September 1986, in response to a ruling in the European Court of Justice that the UK's statutory retirement age discriminates against women (the Marshall ruling), the government has proposed legislation to equalise the retirement ages of men and women. These proposals are contained in the Sex Discrimination Bill introduced in the House of Lords in early 1986.

The Marks and Spencer pension scheme provides for widowers, as well as widows, of former members of staff, and covers part-time workers on a pro-rata basis. Retirement ages are the same as the state ones but staff can retire from the age of 50 onwards, receiving a pension based on age and years of service.

16. Progress Appraisal

Many of the policies so far described amount to little more than good employment practices. But however carefully these recommendations are followed, innate and unconscious prejudice on the part of those influencing personnel decisions can obstruct the fair treatment of women. A firm commitment to equal opportunity can only be realised if all staff are encouraged to examine their own attitudes, and to change them.

Many large organisations maintain formal staff appraisal systems, particularly for management. This system should include an appraisal of each worker's success in terms of the policy outlined in the equal opportunity agreement, as well as their job-related skills.

Equally, the criteria employed in the appraisal system should be revised to ensure that they do not give undue weight to 'masculine' factors such as 'drive and ambition'.

Boots changed its appraisal system in 1985 so as to reduce 'stereotyping' of women, by examining progress in a wider range of skills. Their system also involves an assessment of employees' training and development needs. Other companies have revised the forms used in progress appraisal schemes, in order to improve objectivity, accuracy, and detail. Personnel officers should, of course, be given sufficient training to incorporate the equal opportunities policy into appraisal schemes.

17. Promotion and Transfer

Most of the points made in relation to recruitment of new staff apply equally to promotion and transfer. The jobs to be filled should be examined, and an assessment made as to which qualifications are actually necessary and relevant to the job. Opportunities for promotion and transfer should be advertised throughout the organisation to ensure that all potential candidates are made aware of the vacancies, and that no employees are excluded from consideration because they do not happen to work in the same section or department. In the selection, the characteristics and qualifications required should be carefully defined, so that a realistic judgement can be made about the suitability of potential candidates. Unsuccessful candidates for promotion or transfer should be given reasons for the decision, so that they can improve their future chances.

An annual review system should be used to discuss with employees their progress, future plans (in employment terms) and any training or job opportunities that might benefit them. All staff should be encouraged to take training courses that will help their promotion prospects.

18. Setting Goals and Timetables

Management and employees' representatives should agree on realistic goals for the positive action programme. For example, they could agree that after ten years the proportion of women employed in the technicians' section should have reached at least one third.

This is important as a means of keeping up the momentum, and of ensuring the success of the measures adopted. The goals and timetables agreed should be made public, along with full details of the positive action programme.

If the goals are not reached within the time limits, they will have to be adjusted, as will the strategy for achieving them.

19. Monitoring the Programme

(a) *Set up a joint employee/management working party*. It is important that employees' representatives have an equal say with management in monitoring the progress of positive action. The working party should include employees from all grades and areas of work. It should not be left to the personnel department to monitor the programme, because it will to a large extent be their work which comes under scrutiny. Nor should it be left to union officials and managers — as this will probably exclude women who are supposed to benefit from the scheme.

(b) *Keep written records*. Records of vacancies, promotions, job descriptions, applicants' qualifications, references, shortlists and appointments, including the reasons given for each decision made on appointments, will make it possible to assess the effectiveness of a positive action programme. For example, brief records of interviews will help to ensure that common standards have been applied to all candidates. Records should not include names and addresses of applicants, but only their sex, ethnic origin, and qualifications.

(*c*) *Monitor progress.* Using the original analysis of the workforce, records kept since the programme began, and any other relevant evidence, the working party should review the progress of the positive action programme at least once a year.

(*d*) *Establish a procedure for complaints.* A grievance procedure *must* be agreed between management and unions for individuals who think they have been discriminated against, or who have reason to believe that declared policies for positive action are not being put into practice. It should also be adequate to deal with complaints of sexual and racial harassment.

(*e*) *Adjust the programme if necessary.*

(*f*) *Make sure the agreement is put in writing.* When it has been decided which positive steps are most appropriate to the workplace in question, a written agreement should be drawn up which includes all the details. This may seem an obvious point, but a vaguely-worded positive action programme may be easily side-stepped. It is important that all employees, and all managers, are made aware of the details of the programme, and of management's commitment to implementing it.

Programmes in Operation

This section describes some of the positive action programmes which have been undertaken in the UK in the past 5 years. National agreements between all the unions and employers in a particular industry can be a basic starting point for positive action. One such agreement exists between the Independent Television Companies of the UK and their relevant Unions: the ACTT, NUJ, EETPU and BETA. The agreement covers a wide range of issues and the statement concerning equality of opportunity is as follows:

Equal Opportunities
The parties to this Agreement are committed to the development of positive policies to promote equal opportunity in employment regardless of workers' sex, marital status, creed, colour, race or ethnic origins. This principle shall apply in respect of all conditions of work including pay, hours of work, holiday entitlement, overtime and shift work, work allocation, guaranteed earnings, sick pay, pensions, recruitment, training, promotion, and redundancy.

Below we describe how London's two Independent Television companies, Thames TV and London Weekend TV, have implemented the agreement.

The Thames Television Positive Action Project

In 1977, Thames Television had joined with 37 other major employers in the London Borough of Camden in signing a statement issued by the local Community Relations Council to the effect that they were Equal Opportunity employers. However, no active steps were taken under the legislation to implement this declaration. In 1980, the company was approached by NCCL, who had been funded by the EOC to carry out action research projects in organisations with a view to making recommendations for action under the positive action provisions of the SDA.

Thames agreed to allow Sadie Robarts from the NCCL into the company as an independent researcher to interview women employees and managers to find out what steps would be appropriate for women in the company. The project was carried out during 1980. It was found that Thames, like other television companies, had an employee profile which showed women concentrated into the lower paid, lower graded jobs. The great majority of the women, who represented about 37% of Thames' 2,000 plus workforce, were in the clerical, supervisory or production assistant/researcher jobs. Conversely, men dominated the technical grades such as camera operators and the middle and upper management, whether on the production or administration side. It was also apparent that, while the women in meetings declared an enthusiasm to go into non-traditional jobs such as director or sound engineer, there was no obvious career development path which made it possible for them to do so.

The women divided broadly into three groups: clerical staff who wanted to train as researchers or production assistants; women who wanted to train for non-traditional technician posts; and women researchers and production assistants who wanted opportunities to become producers or directors. In view of these expressed desires, a whole *Programme of Positive Action for Women*, to run initially for five years, was presented to the company. The recommendations included:

1. Appointing a senior executive director to have overall responsibility for implementing the programme.
2. Appointing a women's employment adviser, to be located in the personnel department.
3. Forming a Positive Action Committee comprised of representatives from the unions (BETA, ACTT, NUJ, EETPU), management, non-union staff, and the Women's Committee which had formed during the course of the research.
4. Providing awareness training for managers, and career development courses and advice for women employees.
5. Ensuring that recruitment materials such as advertisements positively encouraged women and did not unintentionally indirectly discriminate in the qualifications that were required for particular jobs.
6. Producing a Code of Practice for the use of managers.
7. Increasing the existing funding for childcare assistance.

Thames agreed to almost all the recommendations, but was at that stage reluctant to attempt to set any targets for improving the representation of women in the managerial or technical grades. The programme of action was begun in late 1981 with considerable internal and external publicity. Over the following four years various steps were taken with a view to widening the opportunities of women employees at Thames, and these are outlined below. The keynote of the company's approach has been to raise awareness and persuade managers that an equal opportunity policy is simply an aspect of good personnel practice, which benefits *all* employees and not just particular groups.

A significant further step was taken early in 1984, when the company widened the programme so that it now has an equal opportunity policy for all employees. The Women's Employment Adviser and the Positive Action Committee were renamed the Equal Opportunities Adviser and the Equal Opportunities Committee, and the recently formed Black and Asian Workers' Committee gained representation on this committee. The first major step under this policy was taken during the autumn of 1985 with the carrying out of a company-wide ethnic monitoring exercise.

Steps taken under the Positive Action Programme include:

1. *The appointment of the Director of Personnel and the Company Secretary* to have overall responsibility for the programme.
2. *Wide publication of the policy* both internally, through the company's magazine, and externally in conferences and by international distribution of the original research report, the equal opportunity booklet, and the code of practice on equal opportunities.
3. *The appointment of a full-time adviser* whose responsibility is to evolve training schemes, provide counselling, and advise and implement the programme on a day-to-day basis.
4. *The establishment of the Equal Opportunities Committee*, which meets on a quarterly basis. Because the members of the Committee represent specific interests, there is informed discussion on matters germane to the Equal Opportunity Policy, the effect of which has been to change the company's practice on certain issues. An example of this was the feeling strongly held by women that if they were applying for posts in other departments, they should not have to inform their manager at least until they were offered an interview. This was because they felt that if they were unsuccessful then their manager might, if unsympathetic, become even more so. After considerable discussion at the Committee, the company agreed to change this practice so that employees do not have to inform their manager of their possible move until they are at the stage of being offered an interview.

66

5. *Childcare assistance* on a limited scale had been provided at Thames Television since 1978. This was increased during 1981 so that at present 6 places are reserved at Kingsway Nursery in central London for Thames employees. At the company's other site at Teddington, financial assistance is provided for whatever childcare arrangements are made by parents, so long as the facility is registered or approved. Parents are given assistance on a sliding scale according to their needs. Consequently, single parents are entitled to the highest rate of assistance as a general rule. Provided mothers have completed 18 months' service with the company, they are entitled to return to work and to 13 weeks' full pay during their maternity leave; their pension contributions are paid throughout their maternity leave up to the statutory 29 weeks. Additionally, the company allows male employees three days paternity leave. The same period is allowed to parents who are adopting children.

Training courses to raise the awareness of managers and to assist women in career development are the most important step under the positive action policy.

Career Development for Women

(*a*) *Television programme familiarisation course.* This course, consisting of eight two-hour evening sessions, was developed in response to women's complaints that even though they might be interested in a technical career (as a camera operator, sound recordist or lighting technician) there was a mystique attached to the equipment and making of a programme which intimidated them from applying for Technical Trainee courses, even if they had appropriate qualifications. The first four sessions are termed 'Elementary' and can be followed up with a second 'Intermediate' block of four evenings. The course allows women to become familiar with the studio and the equipment as it takes them briefly through the steps necessary to make a television programme. By 1985, 200 members of staff had taken the course, of whom three quarters were women.

(*b*) *Basic Science and Technology course.* Because the institutional discrimination of our education system results in fewer girls having 'O' level maths, physics, and other technical subjects, far fewer women are in a position to apply for the company's Technical Trainee course which requires these qualifications. Using the positive action provisions of the SDA, it was possible to design a basic Science and Technology course aimed at women employees. The course was started in 1984 and ran for one evening a week for 12 consecutive weeks. Of the first 12 trainees, two women went on to the full-time Technical Trainee Scheme. Although the course is aimed at women, men can apply, and seven of the fifteen employees who took the course in October 1985 were men.

(c) *Personal effectiveness course.* For women interested in developing themselves as managers, Thames joined with Central Television and the Independent Television Companies Association in sending carefully-selected members of staff on this five-day residential course. For the first course in 1983, a group of 150 women at senior secretarial, supervisory or researcher level were targetted and invited to apply. Of these, 80 applied and over 40 were interviewed. Five women were finally selected, and all felt they had benefited enormously from the course. The Women's Adviser also reported that women who had been interviewed but not selected were pleased to have had the opportunity to discuss their career development.

A total of 54 women participated in further courses over the next three years. Of these, 35 came from clerical and secretarial grades, 7 were managers, and the remainder worked on various aspects of production at researcher level or below. The women's progress was monitored after they had taken the course. By the end of 1985, 61% remained in the same job; 30% had been upgraded, taken on wider responsibilities or taken on a new job in the company; and 9% had left. The courses are being continued jointly with the ITCA in 1986 and an innovation is the inclusion of an additional mixed course.

Awareness Training for Managers

Clearly, under an Equal Opportunity policy, there is no point in developing women's aspirations if their managers are still making recruitment and selection decisions based on stereotypes about the kind of jobs women want or are good at, whether they can lift a video camera, and whether or not they can or should work if they have childcare responsibilities. To avoid this kind of stereotyping, in-house courses on selection and interviewing have been held for managers. Additionally, during 1985, 80 staff, the majority of them managers with responsibility for recruitment decisions, went on a one-day course on Equal Opportunities and Ethnic Monitoring run by an outside consultant. The response to these was generally positive, so that during 1986 follow-up seminars were planned with these managers. The external consultant will be giving half-day courses to other managers and supervisory staff in the future.

Integrating the policy into the work of the Personnel Department is vital if there are to be lasting changes in the employee profile. To this end, work has progressed on rewriting job descriptions to ensure that they do not indirectly discriminate and ensuring that advertisements for jobs are placed in the ethnic minority press. Additionally, during 1985 members of the Personnel Department began to meet on a regular basis so that equal opportunity issues are seen as integral to the work of the Department, and not something which is solely the responsibility of the Equal Opportunity Adviser. Women in the company have sought the advice of the Equal Opportunity Adviser on issues ranging from career development to sexual harassment. It is obviously important that Personnel Officers who are giving such advice are themselves sensitive to equal opportunities considerations and remedies.

Consultation

During the summer of 1985, an extensive consultation exercise took place with managers and supervisors prior to the distribution of forms for self-classification on ethnic origin to all employees. The purpose of this was to reassure staff that the ethnic monitoring information would only be used in the development of positive action for ethnic minorities, and not used in the selection process. The job application form was redesigned with a tear-off self-classification slip so that the numbers of applicants from ethnic minority groups, and their success rate, can be monitored over a period of time.

Equal Opportunities at London Weekend Television

The London Weekend Television policy statement is wider than most Equal Opportunity statements in that it explicitly includes discrimination on the grounds of sexual orientation. The text is set out at the beginning of the Guide to Equal Opportunity Recruitment and selection which has been produced for use by those involved in the recruitment and selection process. The policy is expressed as follows:

LWT Policy

LWT is committed to the development of positive policies to promote equal opportunity in employment regardless of workers' sex, marital status, sexual orientation, disablement, creed, colour, race or ethnic origin. This principle applies in respect of all conditions of work including pay, recruitment, training and promotion.

The policy has been implemented in a number of ways:

1. *Publishing the policy*. This ranges from ensuring that all advertisements include an equal opportunity statement to talks at schools in the London area or professional organisations such as the Industrial Society. There is also a positive policy ensuring that women appear in the visual presentation of programmes which are traditionally dominated by men, such as 'World of Sport'.

2. *Age limits*. Age limits for entry, promotion or training have been removed.

3. *Childcare*. Women employees qualify for maternity leave after 18 months employment. In addition, since 1977 the company has provided financial assistance by funding up to 90% of the cost of up to ten places at Kingsway Nursery in Central London. The assistance is based on the income of the individual employee and does not include that of a partner.

4. *Pension rights*. Men and women, whether full or part-time, are treated on a basis of equality.

5. *Training*. Three voluntary Management Equal Opportunities Awareness Courses have been run. Of the first 26 participants, two were LWT Board members. The one-day courses were run jointly with external trainees and included speakers from the CRE on the importance of ethnic monitoring. The second part of the day was devoted to recruitment, selection and interviewing procedures, and to the importance of recognising indirect discrimination.

Women Only Training. Thirty-three women from LWT have attended a training course on personal effectiveness organised for women in independent television by the Independent Television Companies Association. After the 5-day course, follow-up work was done with the participants, and it was found that over half had gone on to do attachments in other parts of the company, or had started courses outside their working hours. Seven women had widened their responsibilities, and one had become a manager. Participants also expressed interest in more skills-oriented courses and in opportunities for technical training in the television industry.

Attachments. This scheme, which is open to all employees, enables individuals to spend up to six months in another department gaining experience which may assist them in developing a new skill and applying for transfer, promotion or training opportunities. Vacancies for attachments are advertised on company notice boards. Individuals can also apply on their own initiative to departments they wish to be attached to.

6. *Monitoring.* A monitoring exercise of the gender and race profile of the workforce was carried out in 1985. This was implemented only after consultation between management and the unions. As yet, no positive measures have been taken as a result of the information gained during this exercise.

A tear-off self-assessment section on race and ethnic origin is now included in application forms. It is explained to applicants that this section is removed upon receipt of the form to assist in the central analysis of applications by race and sex, and is not seen by those selecting candidates for interview. Early in 1986 the Company planned to establish an Equal Opportunities Committee of approximately 15 members, representing staff, unions and management. The purpose of this will be to assess progress and to discuss the development of the policy.

The Austin Rover Group

Austin Rover Group Ltd. is a subsidiary of the Rover Group plc (formerly BL Ltd.), the state-owned motor vehicle company. It has about 38,000 UK employees, of whom 7% are women. Of the 27,000 hourly graded, or manual workers, some 4.5% are women; and of the 11,000 salaried staff 12.5% are women. These figures are not very informative; but as yet the Company does not publish more detailed information about its workforce.

The motor vehicle industry has been in the doldrums in the UK for some time. Austin Rover, along with other manufacturers, has been running at an operating loss. This, however, was reduced from £26 million in 1984 to £6 million in 1985; and 1985 figures also show that Austin Rover's sales and exports are on the increase.

However, as a result of these economic pressures, the Company has in recent years been largely concerned with ensuring its survival. Recruitment levels have been low, and in this context scope for developing work on equal opportunities has been limited. As the Company's management point out, major initiatives in this area 'had to be delayed in the knowledge that it could be counter-productive to raise expectations if we did not have the resources to allow them to be met.' (Letter to NCCL, 1986)

None the less, in 1976 the Company quickly acknowledged the new equality legislation with its own equal opportunities policy; and in 1985 it took this an important stage further, with an equal opportunity agreement which was negotiated fully with the Trade Unions, and which gained their explicit support.

The Original Equal Opportunities Policy

In 1976, shortly after the Sex Discrimination and Race Relations Acts came into force, Austin Rover issued the following equal opportunities policy:

> The Company's policy and practice require that entry into the Company, and progression within it are determined solely by application of objective criteria and personal merit. No applicant or employee will be treated less favourably than another on grounds of sex, marital status, race, nationality, ethnic or national origin, colour or creed.

> Furthermore no applicant or employee will be placed at a disadvantage by requirements or conditions which have a disproportionately adverse effect on persons of that sex, marital status, race, nationality, ethnic or national origin, colour or creed which cannot be shown to be necessary for the satisfactory performance of the job an applicant seeks or an employee occupies.

This is not a particularly ambitious policy, in that it extends no further than the requirements of the law other than its prohibition of discrimination on grounds of creed; but the Company put considerable effort into publicising it. It was introduced through seminars and circulated to supervisory staff, and it was intended that all employees with managerial responsibilities should eventually receive a half-day's training on it. Employees were told that they were required to observe the provisions of the policy, and that they might be disciplined if they failed to do so. In this sense the policy has the status of any other Company rule.

The Company's Past Record on Equal Opportunity

It is difficult to assess the impact of a policy such as this one, because it sets out to maintain a status quo rather than to change current practices. The lack of detailed information about Austin Rover's workforce also makes it impossible to identify where changes might have taken place.

This lack of information may also make it difficult for a company to defend itself against charges of discrimination. Indeed, Austin Rover and its associate companies in BL Cars Ltd. have several times been found to have contravened the Race Relations Act.

In the early 1980s Industrial Tribunals found evidence of racial discrimination in separate instances at BL Cars plants in West Yorkshire Foundries and Acocks Green; the CRE brought a complaint against the chief security officer at the BL Cowley plant, which was upheld; and at the Castle Bromwich plant (now closed) non-discrimination notices were served both on the Company and on two AUEW shop stewards as a result of a formal investigation by the CRE. Most of these cases were widely publicised, and caused considerable embarrassment to BL. It was in this context that the Austin Rover Group initiated negotiations with the trades unions for a full agreement on equal opportunities within the Company.

Negotiating the Agreement

Given its length and nature, the Equal Opportunity Agreement was negotiated remarkably quickly. The first draft was sent to the Trade Unions concerned in December 1984, and the agreement was formally signed in October 1985. Negotiations were speeded up by the establishment of a small working party, made up of management and lay representatives of both the salaried and the hourly paid workers, which did most of the detailed work. There are two separate union Joint Negotiating Committees (JNCs) one for the salaried staff, and the other for the hourly paid manual workers, and they chose to represent their members separately rather than jointly. The employees' representatives on the working party were therefore elected from within each JNC. Throughout the negotiations issues were referred to the CRE and the EOC for advice and approval. The Trade Unions also made use of TUC resources, particularly for help in understanding the possible implications of different decisions.

The agreement concentrates on the introduction of workforce monitoring, and on establishing a procedure for it: both the management and the unions anticipated difficulties in persuading the workforce to accept this. The management undertook to make a heavy investment in terms of information work and training, and the unions similarly committed themselves to the lengthy task of going through the agreement with their members. Because of the size of the operation, and in order to minimise problems, management insisted on delaying the full implementation of the monitoring programme, and running a pilot scheme at one plant. They chose the Drews Lane plant in Birmingham, on the basis that it was medium-sized, and all the company-wide conditions obtained there.

The pilot was completed in early 1986. Approximately 7% of workers did not fill out the voluntary questionnaire used for monitoring. At the end of the pilot scheme the JNCs accepted recommendations to simplify the information-gathering procedure, but no other significant changes were made.

The Agreement

The agreement was made between the Company, and all the Trade Unions with members working for the Company. There were 12 trade union signatories, representing different sections of the AUEW and TASS, the TGWU, APEX, ASTMS, GMBATU, UCATT, the EETPU and the NSMM. The agreement enlarges on the company's original equal opportunity policy by itemising the joint and separate responsibilities of the Company and the Trade Unions. For example, it specifies that the unions are responsible for avoiding discrimination in admitting members, and in providing their members with access to union facilities and activities. This is not strictly speaking a matter for the Company; its inclusion indicates a considerable measure of good faith on the part of the unions.

The unions also commit themselves to supporting the provision of any training necessary to ensure that the equal opportunity commitment is met. The purpose and scope of the agreement are defined as:

- the promotion and fostering of Equality of Opportunity within the Company;
- the avoidance of discrimination, in accordance with the Equal Opportunity Declaration;
- regular joint monitoring by the Company and Unions of the progress of Equal Opportunity in the Company;
- positive actions to further Equality of Opportunity.

The positive action plans are unspecific. The Company commits itself to regular internal promotion of the agreement and it undertakes to provide training for supervisors and managers in support of it. However, no details are given as to how and when these plans will be put into effect. The Company's reason for this is that they have no preconceived ideas as to where problem areas might be, and they will need to examine the results of their initial monitoring exercise in order to identify their needs.

The Monitoring Programme

Both the Company and the Trade Unions agree that the introduction of employee monitoring is the most important provision of the agreement, and also potentially its least popular feature.

The first stage of the exercise will be to issue all employees with a questionnaire, asking them to categorise themselves according to sex, marital status, parental status, ethnic origin, age, job grade and length of service. This information will be held on computer, and the Company is developing a data system which will enable information on personnel, payroll and training to be linked. The questionnaire is voluntary, but information which is not supplied by an employee will be filled in by their supervisor with the involvement of their Trade Union representative. Employees will be able to check the information that is held about them.

The second, and longer stage of the exercise, will be to record data on all internal and external applicants for jobs with the Company. Job application forms will require little modification for this.

Most of the internal publicity about the agreement has been designed to reassure the workforce about monitoring, and to justify its use. In September 1985 all employees were issued with a communication about the agreement which explained that monitoring would enable the Company to ensure that the equal opportunity policy was 'working as intended'.

The Trade Unions also anticipated possible hostility to monitoring from some sections of the workforce, although the pilot scheme at Drews Lane did not encounter any difficulties. Union representatives have welcomed the exercise, on the basis that it will enable them to prove their case to their members about the need to strengthen equal opportunity practices.

Austin Rover's management see the commitment to monitoring as a radical step, not least because they made it clear to the unions that they intended to use the information collected: they expect monitoring to identify situations where it may be necessary to take disciplinary action against workers who have breached Company policy. The unions do not think that this raises any problems.

Indeed, they insisted that the agreement apply to all Company employees and sub-contractors, and are confident that the existing protection for workers threatened with disciplinary action will not be undermined.

Recruitment

The Company expects the monitoring to reveal under-representation of women and Black people in various job categories. Because there has been very little recruitment in the last ten years, and the current average length of service is 17 years, the present employee profile is a result of recruitment practices dating back to the 1960s. Recruitment is unlikely to rise dramatically, so overall changes will be very gradual. However, much effort has been put into ensuring that where recruitment does take place, the procedures follow the equal opportunity policy. For example, the Company operates the Youth Training Scheme, and has taken positive steps to ensure that schools with high proportions of ethnic minority students are included in their recruitment rounds. The Company also no longer hires the relatives of employees in preference to other applicants.

Grading Structures

Austin Rover overhauled their grading structures in 1978–1980, in order to rationalise them. They are confident that any aspects of the overall structure which might have jeopardised the equal opportunity policy were eliminated at this stage — although that was not the actual purpose of the exercise. They do acknowledge that bargaining separately for hourly-graded and salaried workers can leave employers vulnerable to claims for equal pay for work of equal value: an hourly-graded worker may be in a position to claim equal pay for work of equal value with a salaried worker. However, the Company believes its schemes to be free from bias both within *and* between grading structures.

The Impact of the Equal Opportunity Agreement

Although the Austin Rover agreement is no radical departure from common current practice, it is an important step forward. This is chiefly because of the involvement of the Trade Unions at all stages of its development, and because of the weight attached to these negotiations. The agreement is also the first joint agreement covering both manual and white-collar workers in the Company's history. Similarly, although no major policy shifts are expected, the results of the monitoring programme will enable both unions and management to plan their long-term equal opportunity objectives.

The agreement already has a substantial value as an information-gathering and consciousness-raising exercise. It has been accompanied by a further round of training in equal opportunity practice for all managerial and supervisory staff and Trade Union representatives, which serves both as a reminder of the policy and as an explanation of how this must affect day-to-day work. Guidelines for managers and supervisors have been issued, covering interviewing and selection, and an equal opportunity handbook has also been circulated. All recruitment literature also now gives information about the policy. As a promotional exercise alone, the new agreement will undoubtedly have a significant effect on people's attitudes to, and understanding of, equal opportunity issues: there is potential for it to go much further.

Local Authorities as Purchasers — Contracts Compliance

A substantial amount of the goods and services required by local authorities are purchased from outside contractors. The larger authorities, and in particular the Metropolitan Authorities, have considerable sums of money to spend in this way.

Local authorities are empowered, under the 1972 Local Government Act, to make various requirements of companies wishing to tender contracts with them. Contractors can, of course, decide that the terms specified in a particular contract are unacceptable, and can withdraw their tenders; but if the contract is worth a lot of money to them they will usually prefer to negotiate it. It is this purchasing power which has now been used by some local authorities to ensure that their contractors comply with the laws on equality. The greater the Council's purchasing power, the better chance it has of influencing employment practice in the private sector.

Contracts Compliance and the Equality Laws

All local authorities require certain technical and commercial conditions to be met before a contractor can be put on their 'approved lists'. As a result of Trade Union negotiations, contractors may also be asked to show evidence of good health and safety records, fair wage levels, good practice on Trade Union rights, and high trainee ratios. Companies are accustomed to contracts compliance requirements of this kind.

The principle behind contracts compliance on equal opportunities is the same. Local authorities have a responsibility to set standards in their employment policies, and to protect the interests of those employed, even indirectly, by the authority. Specifically, the RRA requires local authorities to ensure that they carry out their functions with regard to the need to eliminate unlawful discrimination, and to promote equality of opportunity.

A council operating a contracts compliance policy will have had to ensure that its own employment practices meet its standards; ultimately the policy can be used as a sanction, to ensure that public money is channelled only to employers who have similar high standards, and who can show that they comply with the SDA, the RRA and the Disabled Persons Acts. However, local authorities are not permitted to operate law enforcement in the way that the EOC and the CRE are enjoined to: where a contractor fails to comply with the authority's equal opportunity requirements — as with its health and safety requirements — the sanction is exclusion from the approved lists, rather than enforcement.

The Greater London Council's Contracts Compliance Policy

In 1983 the GLC and the Inner London Education Authority (ILEA) adopted a contracts compliance policy, and the GLC set up a Contracts Compliance and Equal Opportunities Unit (CCEOU) to supervise its implementation. The Council had imported this idea from the USA, where the Federal Government, employing almost a third of the country's workforce, has operated such a policy since the mid-1960s. (See p. 106.)

1. The GLC's Purchasing Powers

The GLC first had to assess where its policy could have most influence. In 1983 it estimated its annual external purchases of goods and services to total £700 million. It examined its accounts in order to identify where this money was spent and to find out who held its largest contracts. It then informed all of the companies on its approved lists about the Contracts Compliance policy, and drew their attention to the new Equal Opportunities clause in its Code of Practice on Tenders and Contracts.

2. The Equal Opportunities Clause

This clause was based on the CRE and EOC Codes of Practice:

The Council requires all companies engaged in providing goods and services to take all reasonably practicable steps to ensure:

78

1. the widest possible response from all sections of the community to employment opportunities within the company and that all potential applicants receive equal encouragement to apply;
2. that no job applicant/employee receives less favourable treatment or is placed at a disadvantage on grounds which are not job-related (e.g., race, sex, disability etc.);
3. that all employees are treated fairly and equally with respect to terms and conditions of service, allocation of work, promotion, transfer and training opportunities within the company;
4. that there is progress towards a fair representation of women and ethnic minorities at all levels throughout the workforce;
5. that appropriate arrangements are made to review regularly, and evaluate the company's progress in achieving equal opportunities.

3. The Review of Companies

The GLC's next step was to establish priorities for reviewing the 20,000 companies on its lists. These priorities take account of the size of the contract, trade union organisation within the company, and its workforce profile. For instance, in the Supplies Department the companies chosen for review in 1983 were those with whom the Council had spent more than £50,000 in 1982. Large companies were selected rather than small ones because the policy would then affect a larger workforce. The CCEOU also decided to review companies about which it had received complaints of discriminatory practices.

Companies under review were asked to fill out an application form for retention or inclusion on the GLC's lists. The form asked for information about the composition of the company's workforce by gender, ethnic origin, and grade of job, as well as details about particular employment practices. Companies who refused to fill out the questionnaire at all were recommended by the CCEOU for exclusion from the GLC's approved lists.

The information returned on the application forms was assessed by the CCEOU and employers were interviewed and given advice about the equal opportunity policies and practices necessary to bring them into compliance with the GLC's requirements. They were also given help in devising and timetabling their own positive action programmes. Companies who failed to negotiate and agree on a programme were again recommended for debarment, although the CCEOU emphasised at all stages that its preference was to bring them into compliance with the policy.

4. The Impact of the Policy

In the USA contracts compliance is carried out by the Federal Government, and all contractors are obliged to co-operate with it. The GLC had no such powers of enforcement: it had to rely entirely on its financial clout and its powers of persuasion to influence contractors. Its commercial influence did not extend to large companies for whom the GLC contract was insignificant: for example, in 1984 Rowntree Mackintosh declined to complete the CCEOU's questionnaire, presumably because they did not consider that the size of the contract justified the effort, and were debarred. Similarly, companies with a monopoly on a specialist service or product were immune to commercial pressures from the GLC if it could not do without their services.

Most companies, however, agreed to provide the CCEOU with information, and welcomed the advice and assistance they were offered. David Dolton, Assistant General Manager of NEM Business Services Ltd., commented in February 1986 at a GLC Symposium on Contracts Compliance that his company had been glad of the CCEOU's expertise in helping them to tackle a perceived management problem. There is considerable value to management in being seen to have good employment practices.

The CCEOU began its work with a review of the building companies on the approved lists held in the Architects' Department. From the inception of the policy until December 1985, 106 companies were selected for detailed investigation. By that time, 77 had agreed to undertake specified programmes of action to bring them in line with the GLC's requirements. A further 17 were still negotiating these programmes; and 12 had been debarred from the list. Of these 12, nine had refused to provide information or meet with the CCEOU, and three had failed to meet the requirements of other GLC departments.

The role of contracts compliance in the UK is thus far an educative one: it consists of advising employers as to the terms of the law, and as to how they can ensure that they meet these terms. The CCEOU found the level of knowledge and understanding amongst employers about equal opportunity policy and practice to be unexpectedly low, and thus spent more time than was originally envisaged in assisting them and monitoring their progress.

The GLC had a qualified success in meeting its principal objectives, which were to introduce into the private sector some of the better equal opportunity practices which had been developed in the public sector, by bringing companies into compliance. However, largely because the policy had no powers of enforcement, the

Council had to debar a higher proportion of companies than expected. Debarment represented a failure of the contracts compliance policy.

Following the abolition of the GLC in March 1986 the CCEOU was taken over by the Inner London Education Authority (ILEA), who were already operating contracts compliance with the GLC. However, the ILEA's purchasing power is substantially smaller than that of the GLC, and the policy cannot be expected to continue to have the same impact.

5. The Implications for Central Government

Contracts Compliance would be more effective if it were operated by central government, and extended to all government contractors, (as it is in the USA) because the legal and financial sanctions would be greater. At present, however, government emphasis is on privatisation rather than on intervention in the market. The Local Government Planning and Land Act 1980 requires local authority DLOs to compete with the private sector for contracts with the authority. Proposals to extend these measures to other local authority services were published in a 1985 Government Green Paper, *Competition in the provision of local authority services.*

As well as proposing further local authority privatisation, the Green Paper recommends measures to restrict local authorities from making any requirements of contractors which are not directly related to the work to be done — its quality, timing or cost. This is intended 'to promote the extension of free competition in the provision of local authority services'. Contracts compliance is perceived in some government and business quarters as interfering with this free competition. Although nothing has resulted from this Green Paper, similar proposals in the future could jeopardise contracts compliance policies operated at local government level. This is because, although the measures should not affect a contractor's duty to comply with statutory requirements such as those on health and safety or sex discrimination, they could certainly inhibit the authority from examining a contractor's record on complying with these requirements.

Nonetheless, there is some interest on the part of central government in contracts compliance as a remedy for job discrimination. There is increasing documentation of racial discrimination both in the job market and on training schemes, and the government is under some pressure to be seen to be tackling this. In October 1985 David Waddington, a Minister in the Home Office, announced that he was examining the possibilities of a government initiative on contracts compliance: this was in the wake

81

of a series of violent confrontations between the police and Black people in London and Birmingham. The Department of Employment subsequently rejected Mr. Waddington's suggestions, but may yet adopt these or similar measures in order to affirm its commitment to combatting racial discrimination.

This would not necessarily improve employment opportunities for women; indeed, the interests of Black women are not automatically secured by programmes to combat either race discrimination *or* sex discrimination. The GLC, however, by combining its anti-discrimination programmes in the work of a single Unit, attempted to avoid such pitfalls.

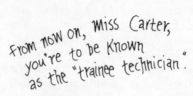

From now on, Miss Carter, you're to be known as the "trainee technician".

The Trade Unions

The Trade Unions have the key role to play in negotiating for equal opportunities and for enforcement of the equality laws. They were set up, not simply to defend their members' statutory rights, but also to negotiate for improvements to their legal entitlements. Thus, where the law is inadequate, the unions can try to establish rights for workers through collective bargaining. The Transport and General Workers' Union's women's handbook says: 'the law should be seen as a safety net, not a substitute for collective bargaining'. Although many of the examples we have used in this book are of positive action measures which have been initiated by management, a policy which has been instigated by the Trade Unions in a workplace is bound to be both stronger and more effective. This is, firstly, because a policy which has the agreement of the entire workforce has a much better chance of success at every level; whereas a policy imposed by management without the consent of the workers' representatives may well meet with incomprehension and obstruction.

Secondly, the Trade Unions are in a much better position than management to understand and fully appreciate the needs and interests of their members, and therefore to gain their support on policy issues.

Thirdly, and perhaps most importantly, the Trade Unions have the interests of their members as a first priority. A positive action programme introduced by management without negotiation can easily be adjusted or even removed entirely to suit the interests of the management. A policy negotiated through the unions, however, is more likely to reflect the needs of the workforce.

This is not to say that the Trade Union Movement as a whole has embraced anti-discrimination measures as the priority issues they should be. On the contrary, we have yet to see the majority of Trade Unions mounting an effective challenge to the iniquities of job segregation and pay disparity among their membership. Recent years have seen extensive job losses and a consequent fall in membership for many unions; and the protection of jobs and industries has inevitably taken precedence. For many trade unionists this means protecting *men's* jobs, and thereby defending the 'family wage'. Challenging sex discrimination — and racism — is often, in this context, seen as irrelevant.

Nonetheless, substantial progress has been made in some Trade Unions. Changes have taken place, and precedents have been set, in terms both of collective bargaining practice and of women's representation within trade union structures. This section is not intended to review the Trade Union Movement as a whole, but to describe initiatives taken in individual unions, and explain how they were brought about.

Women's Participation in the Unions

Since the turn of the century women have been joining Trade Unions at a faster rate than men. In 1985 they made up approximately 33% of the total Trade Union membership. This growth is associated with the growth of unionisation in white-collar jobs, and also with the growth of the service sectors which employ women.

However, the proportion of women members still does not reflect their numbers in the workforce; nor is it reflected in their representation on executive councils, among full-time officials, and among delegates to the Trades Union Congress. (see Table 4 below)

Table 4   Representation of Women in Trade Unions
January 1985

Union	Membership		Executive members	Full-time officials	TUC delegates
	Total	% women	% women	% women	% women
APEX	95,049	53.2	20.0	4.2	38.5
ASTMS	390,000	22.5	9.1	6.3	10.7
BIFU	154,579	50.9	12.5	19.0	21.0
CPSA	190,347	72.2	13.8	21.4	30.0
GMBATU	766,744	33.7	2.6	4.1	4.6
NALGO	766,390	51.0	28.1	10.4	31.9
NUPE	680,000	67.0	38.5	6.6	29.4
NUT	250,499	71.9	19.5	7.4	27.0
NUTGW	76,509	90.6	53.3	10.5	77.0
TGWU	1,490,555	15.3	2.4	1.8	9.8
USDAW	392,307	61.0	5.5	8.1	14.3

There are specific provisions in the SDA for Trade Unions to take positive action to increase women's participation. These include targetted recruitment, special training for women, and reserved seats (see page 5). Increasing numbers of unions are voting to use these powers. However, equal representation — although desirable — is not an end in itself. The essential point is that women's needs should inform the unions' priorities, and their demands should be part of the unions' demands of management.

The TUC first adopted policy on equal pay in 1888, but this issue, along with other crucial issues for women at work, has only recently gained any prominence in trade union demands.

There is currently some debate amongst women trade unionists as to whether increasing the numbers of women executive members and union officers is the best way of making the unions work for women. It is often argued that change in the unions' priorities will only come about if women occupy their share of the most powerful positions in the union hierarchies. This view is frequently challenged, however, on the basis that changes at the top are merely cosmetic, and rarely trickle down to the ordinary membership. Women who reach the top in a male-dominated union will also have had to conform to established ideas and principles of trade unionism.

Unions have taken very different approaches to these issues: in some instances this has included a degree of separate organisation, and the holding of special women's conferences.

Black Women in the Unions

The RRA allows Trade Unions to take positive action to increase the participation of people from ethnic minority groups. Most unions, however, do not collect information about the ethnic origins of their members, and they are therefore unable to put such information to use.

There are signs that the Trade Union Movement is taking some initiatives on race equality. Measures have included the setting up of working parties to examine measures to combat racism and racial discrimination; the translation of trade union courses and publications into minority languages; and the adoption of anti-racist policies.

Progress for one group of workers often accompanies progress for another, and demands for racial equality in the unions have certainly coincided with demands for sex equality. However, women and Black activists have not always worked in unison, in spite of the fact that Black women are among the lowest paid in the workforce. The Trade Union Movement has yet to set up a satisfactory structure for ensuring co-operation between people working on equality issues, but there is increasing recognition of the need for unity.

The TUC

The TUC has held an annual women's conference since 1931, in recognition that the Trade Union Movement was neglecting to defend the interests of women members. There is also a Women's Officer and a twenty-member TUC Women's Advisory Committee. Neither this Committee nor the women's conference has any executive powers. The conference is intended to raise issues which might otherwise be ignored, and its resolutions are passed on to the TUC General Council: but the TUC has no obligation to enforce them. Repeated calls for the Women's TUC to have a wider remit and greater powers have so far had little impact.

The Women's TUC does have some input, however. In 1979 the TUC adopted the following ten-point Charter for positive action for women in the unions:

1. The National Executive Committee of the union should publicly declare to all its members the commitment of the union to involving women members in the activities of the union at all levels.

2. The structure of the union should be examined to see whether it prevents women from reaching the decision-making bodies.

3. Where there are large women's memberships but no women on the decision-making bodies, special provision should be made to ensure that women's views are represented, either through the creation of additional seats or by co-option.

4. The National Executive Committee of each union should consider the desirability of setting up advisory committees within its constitutional machinery to ensure that the special interests of its women members are protected.

5. Similar committees at regional, divisional, and district level could also assist by encouraging the active involvement of women in the general activities of the union.

6. Efforts should be made to include in collective agreements provision for time off without loss of pay to attend branch meetings during working hours where that is practicable.

7. Where it is not practicable to hold meetings during working hours every effort should be made to provide child-care facilities for use by either parent.

8. Child-care facilities, for use by either parent, should be provided at all district, divisional and regional meetings and particularly at the union's annual conference, and for training courses organised by the union.

9. Although it may be open to any member of either sex to go to union training courses, special encouragement should be given to women to attend.

10. The content of journals and other union publications should be presented in non-sexist terms.

The TUC also reserves 5 places on its General Council for women; but the remaining 41 seats are all held by men. Nonetheless, the General Council has over the past 10 years endorsed increasingly progressive policies on women's rights; although these have not necessarily been transformed into concerted positive action, there is an increasing *policy* commitment to fighting for equal opportunities.

The National Union of Public Employees (NUPE)

The huge expansion of public services in the 1960s brought about a significant increase in women's employment, and a consequent increase in the female membership of NUPE. In 1985, there were 455,000 women in NUPE — 67% of the total membership. Women members are concentrated in the Health Service, as nurses, ancillary workers and health visitors; in school catering and cleaning services; and in local government services.

The Warwick Report

In 1974 the Local Government, Health and Water Services were reorganised, and NUPE commissioned a report from Warwick University to investigate the steps the Union would have to take in order to adapt to these changes.

As well as recommending organisational changes in the Union, the Warwick Report argued for changes in the 'very attitudes and philosophy underlying the Union's overall structure'; and in particular it highlighted the underrepresentation of women in the

Union. At this point there had never been a woman full-time officer or Executive Council member in NUPE.

Representation of Women in NUPE

A Special National Conference in 1975 voted to establish 5 reserved seats for women on the National Executive Council, in addition to the 21 existing seats; it also created 2 additional women's seats on each of the 11 Divisional Councils, bringing their numbers up to 16 each.

However, by 1982 it was apparent that these changes at the Executive level had not remedied the under-representation of women at branch level, and there was also concern that branches were unrepresentative in general. The 1982 National Conference called on the Executive Council to institute a policy of 'positive discrimination', and as a result a National Women's Working Party (now known as the National Women's Advisory Committee) was set up, and a National Women's Officer appointed. Additionally, each of NUPE's Divisions set up a Women's Advisory Committee. These initiatives at Divisional level were an effort to ensure that policy changes had a local impact: there is little evidence to suggest that appointments to the Executive would in themselves have made any difference to most women in NUPE, even if they had heard about them.

The 1984 Trade Union Act, which required unions to hold secret ballots of their membership in certain circumstances, allowed for non-active members to influence their unions' policy-making. It is debatable whether this actually increases democracy within the Trade Union Movement, but it has certainly increased the size of the ballot within unions, and must therefore have increased the women's vote. The result of making attendance at branch meetings a precondition for involvement in union matters has often in the past been the virtual exclusion of women: particularly women with children who cannot attend meetings outside working hours.

The Women's Working Party Report

The NUPE Women's Working Party bore this in mind when presenting its report to the Executive Council in 1984. This report made extensive recommendations to the Union to increase women's opportunities. On the issue of women's poor attendance at branch meetings, the report pointed out that women had been in the forefront of recent industrial action, and that the branch structure prevented women from getting involved. It recommended that branches negotiate for time off with pay for meetings, or that they provide for childcare if those negotiations were unsuccessful; and that they organise transport to and from branch meetings. It also pointed out that holding meetings in pubs or clubs would exclude Asian women. Smaller section meetings were proposed, to increase contact within each branch, and it was also suggested that a more informal atmosphere at meetings, and a rotating chair, would encourage more women to take part. Branches were advised to elect Women's Liaison Officers, to ensure communication between the Women's Advisory Committees and the membership. The Women's Working Party expressed concern at the way in which the women's structure in NUPE was being built from the top down, and said:

We are not aiming to establish women's seats and women's committees just for the sake of setting up more committees. We do not want yet another burden to be placed on the same women who have always been involved. The questions are how we get more women involved, how we get proper representation of women and of the occupations where women are in the majority (e.g. school meals, nursing) and how we get the particular perspective of women into the forefront of our thinking and the mainstream of the Union's work.

This 'particular perspective', argued the report, would necessarily include social and political issues of concern to women:

the development and quality of the public services is not only a question of paid employment but also a major factor in the domestic lives of women which may enable us or not to seek paid employment in the first place and determine the type of job and hours we can do.

There is a direct link between the deterioration of public provision and the domestic demands made on women workers. Furthermore, because of the nature of their work, there is substantial resistance from many NUPE members to taking effective industrial action.

NUPE has responded to the increasing privatisation of public services, such as hospital cleaning, by supporting in-house tenders. Although this protects some existing jobs, it involves the Union in negotiating for reductions in hours and some loss of jobs. This has had a disproportionate impact on women, and has been a very controversial practice.

In this context, the protection of standards at work — usually seen as a management priority — has become a key issue for the Union, on a par with and linked to the protection of jobs. Without this central commitment, the Union's focus on women's issues might well be seen as threatening men's jobs.

Priorities for Women in Collective Agreements

NUPE has an impressive campaigning record on the issue of low pay and, by extension, that of equal pay. It has fought for a statutory minimum wage, set at two-thirds of the average male manual worker's wage, and has supported improvements to the Equal Pay Act, including the Equal Value Amendment.

The NHS ancillary pay structure has 18 grades, with women concentrated in the lowest two. Overtime and bonus payments represent a significant proportion of men's wages: many women do not qualify for bonuses and cannot fit in any overtime, and the Union has increasingly recognised this in its national negotiations. The 1982 Conference called for the elimination of the lowest 3 grades, and a revision of the grading system on equal value principles.

NUPE has also argued for flat-rate pay increases to protect low-paid workers; for increased shift payments, which would help reduce the pay disparity between men and women; for protection for part-time workers; and for substantial reductions in working hours. Agreements on childcare provision and on parental leave cannot yet be said to be a priority in negotiations; but the National Women's Advisory Committee has pointed out that a major reduction in working hours for men will pave the way for far-reaching social change, in the form of increased participation by men in domestic responsibilities.

The Race Equality Working Party

The NUPE Race Equality Working Party was set up in 1984, and presented its report to the Executive Council in 1985.

Its recommendations included measures to increase ethnic minority participation in the Union, and to combat racism and racial harassment. The Working Party decided against recommending the appointment of a full-time Race Equality officer, agreeing instead that the lay membership of a Race Equality Advisory Committee should be invested with the responsibility for national initiatives. This Committee was set up early in 1986 and has facilities for some input into Executive Council decisions: discussions are taking place with the National Women's Advisory Committee about how the two Committees can co-ordinate their efforts and tackle common problems.

Education

Trade Union education is seen as a key factor in increasing members' participation in NUPE. Women's Trade Union schools can provide members with the experience and confidence to become active in the Union. In 1982 the Union resolved to provide specialised women's courses in all of its Divisions. Previously these were restricted to members holding branch positions, but they are now open to all women members. The Women's Advisory Committee is also monitoring the take-up of general union courses, to ensure that women are not under-represented, and is producing an education pack for women.

Progress

Significant progress has been made in improving women's representation in the Union. In 1974, women comprised 28% of all shop stewards: 10 years later this figure had grown to 42%. By 1986, eleven of the 28 Executive Council members were women, five of them in reserved seats, and six out of the 11 Divisions had women full-time officers.

At a time when other public service unions have been losing membership, NUPE has been gaining, and the National and Divisional Women's Advisory Committees have seen the recruitment of women workers as a major priority. This has undoubtedly given them greater negotiating power within the Union.

The Electrical, Electronic, Telecommunications and Plumbing Union (EETPU)

Of the EETPU's 400,000 strong membership, approximately 10% are women, and they are concentrated in semi-skilled factory jobs in engineering and telecommunications, and in white-collar, clerical, technical and administrative jobs. White-collar workers are represented by the Electrical and Engineering Staff Association (EESA).

The growth of new technologies has opened up new areas of female employment, in industries which are relatively under-unionised and where numbers of workers are on short-term, part-time or temporary contracts. The electronics industries are subject to considerable fluctuation, and are extensive employers of women in the more dispensable and vulnerable jobs. Under these circumstances it is more difficult for Trade Unions to recruit members, and to keep them in membership. However, the EETPU's membership has been changing, partly as a result of job losses amongst semi-skilled workers in the traditional electrical and mechanical industries, and it has perceived that the new technologies will furnish much of the potential growth in union membership.

The Representation of Women in EETPU

In 1982 the Union appointed a full-time women's officer; and in 1985 the Executive Council endorsed a statement on equal opportunities, and set up an Equal Opportunities Committee.

Owing to the concentration of women in a few sex-segregated areas of work, the numbers of women shop stewards do roughly reflect the proportion of women in EETPU. However, there are no women on the Executive Council; and out of 110 full-time officials there are only 2 women.

The Equal Opportunities Committee

The Executive Council's equal opportunities statement commented:

Women have long formed a substantial part of EETPU & EESA membership, working in an ever-increasing range of occupations and industries. In order to fully represent these members, our policies and activities must reflect their priorities and concerns. The greater the involvement of women in the Union at all levels, the more likely this is to happen.

The appointment of a Women's Officer has enabled work in this area to develop. There is a regular Women's Bulletin and specialist Shop Steward Training Courses at the Union's colleges and, on request, in-plant. Information and assistance is available to all Union members. The Union has also done a considerable amount to publicize recent changes in the equal pay law, leading to a number of cases being taken through negotiation around the country.

The Equal Opportunities Committee was established to ensure a 'comprehensive regional and industrial input' to the Union's equal opportunities work. It is a small committee, comprising an Executive member, the women's officer, and 6 lay members. It is responsible for furthering the Union's anti-racist work as well as its policy on women's issues. It is intended to be a decision-making body — although it has to refer most issues to the Executive Council — and the decision to appoint lay members was to ensure that there was a regular branch-level contribution. One of the Committee's first decisions was to turn the very popular 18-month-old Women Worker's Bulletin into an Equal Opportunities Bulletin: much emphasis is placed on the need to tackle all forms of discrimination within a general framework of equal opportunities. As yet, however, there is no Race Equality officer and there are no Black full-time officials.

The bulletin covers a wide range of issues, including part-time work, pensions, health and safety, and news of current negotiations; it also provides information about non-union issues which may concern members.

The Committee resolved that all the Union's education provision — shop stewards' courses, negotiating courses and industrial law courses — should have an equal opportunities component, not just the specialist courses. Education is one of its priorities, as are equal pay for work of equal value, racial discrimination in the Youth Training Scheme, and equal access to apprenticeships.

The EESA has a separate Equal Opportunities Working Party with similar responsibilities.

Collective Bargaining

The Union's Equal Opportunities Committee, because it runs parallel to the negotiating committees rather than feeding into them, has no automatic impact on negotiating practice. It maintains that changes in negotiating priorities will only result from women's direct involvement; and that, although policy commitments to equal opportunities are necessary, they will not in themselves affect negotiating practices.

At the same time, the Committee through its bulletin gives prominence to news of negotiations, on the basis that women will start to get involved when they see that the Union is working on areas that immediately affect them.

The EETPU has been involved in a number of equal pay negotiations on behalf of its members. In 1985 women members at Baldwin and Francis, a Manchester factory, successfully used the equal value amendment to the Equal Pay Act to negotiate equal pay with higher-paid male colleagues; they were given assistance by job evaluation experts and shop stewards from the EETPU. At GEC Xpelair, the semi-skilled women workers won parity of bonus earnings with the semi-skilled men, again with Union support. Union officials have also been steering a number of equal pay claims through the internal job appraisal committee at Warner Electrics in Bishop Auckland.

The EESA has also negotiated agreements which have a particular impact on women. At Currys Mastercare Ltd, it has negotiated for all women in the company to be screened regularly for cancer at the expense of the company.

The Union has produced literature about health and safety and equal pay issues, which has had a very favourable response from members.

Education

Since 1982 the EETPU has provided for members to attend women-only shop steward training courses. This is seen as a necessary temporary measure to ensure that enough women get the training: since it is pressure from shop stewards and activists that affects union policy, it is vital that women are involved in putting on this pressure.

There are also courses available on specific issues, such as equal pay, parental rights at work, the protective legislation for women workers, and the Sex Discrimination Act; and there are courses on trade union negotiating and policy which are geared towards women members.

Progress

Although women are a minority in the EEPTU, their concentration in clerical and assembly work has enabled them to have a significant impact on some Union policies. They have chosen to concentrate on how the Union tackles workplace issues rather than on getting reserved seats on the Executive Council or other major structural changes. The gradual expansion of the Union's priorities to take account of its women members has borne out this approach.

The National Union of Tailors and Garment Workers (NUTGW)

The NUTGW currently has 80,000 members, of whom 90% are women. A large proportion of the Union's potential membership is employed in the wages council sector and, increasingly, as homeworkers. Since 1979 there have been huge job losses in the industry, primarily in factories, where the Union is most organised. In the years from 1979 to 1982 the Union's membership fell by one third.

Representation of Women

Trade Union organisation is extremely difficult in an industry with so many small factories and homeworkers. Male members have tended to be in the best-paid jobs in the industry, and have correspondingly dominated the Union's affairs. Over the past 5 years, however, this has been changing rapidly. In 1981 75% of the delegates at the National Conference were women; in 1985 this figure had increased to 80%. In 1981, also, 6 women were elected to the 15-strong Executive Board, formerly almost all-male. Branches are now encouraged to ensure that their nominations to the Executive Board reflect the make-up of the Union.

Currently all 7 Divisional officers are male, and only 5 of the 36 full-time offices are held by women. However, a 1985 policy change at branch level, resulting from an Executive decision, is gradually increasing the extent of women's involvment throughout the Union. Branches were quite clearly disorganised and were functioning ineffectively, if at all: a report in 1975 showed that many of them were not even holding meetings.

The Executive decision was to reorganise branch meetings, holding them during working hours rather than in the evenings, and to set up branch committees. These are made up of shop stewards as opposed to members who happen to be able to attend meetings, and as such they are more representative. Attendance at Union meetings has increased a great deal, and in a Union with such a high proportion of women members this is a clear indication that women are better able to participate. It also shows that in a comparatively small Union with a large number of women, minor structural changes can have a major impact.

Union Policy

The NUTGW does not publish its own literature on women's issues, and it has done very little to address the specific needs of its large ethnic minority membership. However, it does circulate TUC literature, and it takes part in the work of a national alliance of groups concerned with the rights of homeworkers.

Again, the Union has not yet explored the potential for equal pay claims for its women members. The general climate in the industry is obviously hostile to improving conditions of work, and in the context of widespread factory closures the pursuit of job evaluation and pay claims has seemed too risky. The Union has supported campaigns to improve the Equal Pay Act from the outset, and has also sought for better health and safety regulations and the maintenance of the legislation protecting women factory workers.

The National Union of Journalists (NUJ)

The NUJ has approximately 33,000 members, of whom one-third are women: the proportion of women members is gradually increasing.

Representation of Women in the NUJ

In 1972 the Annual Delegate Meeting of the Union set up a committee on equality, which became the Equality Working Party in 1975. This Working Party conducted a survey in 1982 on the level of women's participation in the Union, and found, predictably, that women were significantly under-represented in their branches, although every bit as interested as men in Union affairs. The under-representation worsened further up the Union hierarchy: there were only 2 women full-time officials and 2 women on the National Executive Council.

The Equality Council

In 1983 the Equality Working Party became the Equality Council. This has 14 members, 7 representing the Union's industrial sectors and 7 nominated by branches and elected by the members. The Council's responsibilities are set out in the Union's Rule Book:

• Monitoring the progress of relevant legislation and campaigning for improvements when necessary:

- Opposing and publicising where possible cases of sex-based discrimination within the Union and promoting equality in the Union.

- Campaigning against sexism in the media; and

- Encouraging the formation of pro-equality groups within the Union and liaising with pro-equality groups and chapel and branch equality officers.

Since 1983, all Union branches and chapels have also been required by rule to have equality officers, and special courses for these officers are run twice yearly. The NUJ also runs a women officers course, as well as regular dayschools. The function of the branch and chapel equality officers is to promote equality issues in negotiations, and to advise on Union policy locally.

The Equality Council has published a series of leaflets and booklets covering such things as job-sharing, sexual harassment, parental leave, equal pay and positive action. These guidelines explain the Union's policy, describe how individual chapels have implemented it, and include model agreements for negotiation.

In 1985 the NUJ appointed a full-time officer with responsibility for all aspects of equality. In addition, the Union holds an annual Women's Conference, which in 1985 focused on encouraging women to take up offices in chapels, branches, on the Industrial Councils and on the Executive.

The Code of Conduct

The NUJ has always been notable in its endeavours to publicise equality issues within the Union, and to influence the manner in which journalists actually do their jobs. Clause 10 of the NUJ Code of Conduct says:

> Journalists shall only mention a person's race, colour, creed, illegitimacy, marital status (or lack of it), gender or sexual orientation if this information is strictly relevant. A journalist shall neither originate nor process material which encourages discrimination on any of the above-mentioned grounds.

In 1985 the Equality Council set up a 'Campaign for Real People', to combat media stereotyping of women, Black people, people with disabilities, lesbians, gay men, and older people. This campaign has been accompanied by a series of leaflets for journalists explaining how to avoid discriminatory reporting; the Equality Council has also produced literature with suggestions for avoiding sexism in reporting, which asks journalists to 'try the double standard test — would you use this description of a man?'

Even a cursory glance at the news-stands shows how slight the impact of this campaign has been; but it is certainly the most strenuous and concerted effort made by any union to determine anti-discriminatory standards of behaviour for its members. Other professional unions include guidelines on anti-racism and anti-sexism in their codes of conduct; but the NUJ has a structure for dealing with complaints, and it makes active efforts to enforce the Code and can discipline members who break it.

The Ethics Council

In 1985 the Annual Delegate Meeting agreed to set up an Ethics Council to promote and enforce professional and ethical standards, and to deal with, amongst other things, complaints relating to the Code of Conduct, and to enforce the code through Union chapels. Complaints may be made by NUJ branches, NUJ members or indeed members of the public.

The Race Relations Working Party

The NUJ set up a sub-committee on race relations in 1974, which became the NEC Working Party in 1980. It has 7 members, five of them elected by the Annual Delegate Meeting and two elected by the Executive. Currently it is looking at ways of ensuring that equality officers in branches and chapels include race issues as part of their brief. It has also set up meetings around the country for members to discuss racism in reporting, and access for Black people to the media. It intends to produce a membership profile of the Union in order to monitor the needs and priorities of Black members. The NUJ has recently started monitoring the profile of new Union members and hopes eventually that the membership profile will be undertaken of all members, which will enable the Union to more effectively meet the needs and priorities of Black members.

Trade Union Negotiations

The Equality Council has produced a range of literature on negotiating for equality, and it publicises good agreements. Because there are equality officers throughout the union structure, the resources exist to ensure a wide dissemination of this information. The Union has also ruled that there should be an equality officer present on any negotiating team, making sure that equality issues are included in every house claim.

The Equality Council acknowledges that this rule can be difficult to enforce, and that equality demands are often the first to be sacrificed in union negotiations. However, the groundwork has been laid for negotiations for better parental leave, childcare facilities, part-time workers' rights and job-sharing facilities. Some advances have been made: Haymarket/VNU Magazines have agreed to pay £45 a month towards childcare for children under school age; and Penguin Books have agreed to 52 weeks maternity leave, 20 of them on full pay. The Financial Times has a number of posts which are job-shared.

Progress

Rather than reserving seats for women on its Executive, the NUJ has set up a separate equality structure with some authority within the Union. This has given the Union's policy on women's issues considerable prominence and, indeed, some impact. The participation of women in Union matters has also been gradually increasing. In 1980 there was one woman on the National Executive. Union posts may now be job-shared, and in 1985, out of a total of 28 Executive members, 6 were women, 2 posts were job-shared.

The National and Local Government Officers' Association (NALGO)

NALGO has over 750,000 members, just over half of whom are women. It represents white collar workers in a diverse range of services, from local government and the Health Service to the water, gas and electricity services. However, the bulk of its membership works in local government — an area of employment which has seen major managerial initiatives on equal opportunities. The willingness of a few employers in local government to introduce effective positive action programmes has raised important issues for the Trade Union Movement: NALGO has had to define its relationship to specific and detailed proposals for change, as opposed simply to expressing its general support for reform.

Women's Participation in the Union

NALGO was one of the first unions to start providing childcare facilities at annual conferences and other Union meetings, and there is a long-standing policy that branch meetings should be held at lunchtimes or during working hours. However, the Union has chosen not to reserve seats for women on its National Executive Council, and women activists in the Union argue that to do so would distract people from the real issues of Union policy. Equally, they argue that providing creches and other facilities to enable women to come to meetings does not in itself increase attendance levels. The value of such practices is that they show the Union's commitment to involving its women members.

Without reserved seats, women are gradually increasing their representation on the Executive Council. In the 5 years to 1985, women's share of the Executive seats, currently 71 in number, increased from one-fifth to one-third.

The issue of reserved seats

Women in some other unions argue that the issue of reserved seats on the Executive is a red herring. In 1982, women in the Association of Cinematograph, Television and Allied Technicians (ACTT) decided not to ask for reserved seats, because until then no women were standing for election to the general seats: it was agreed to put forward women candidates, and return to the question of reserved seats only if they were unsuccessful. In the event, women did get elected to the general seats, and they now hold approximately 35% of the places on the Executive — which is higher than their proportion of the membership.

Women activists further argue that establishing reserved seats can actually restrict women's activities in their unions, by institutionalising them. In 1984 the NUPE Women's Working Party, whilst agreeing that their existing 5 reserved seats were necessary, argued against increasing this number on the grounds that women would then be even more unlikely to stand for the general seats. They also proposed that women should be allowed to serve for a limited period only in the reserved seats, before moving into the open competition for the general seats. This was on the basis that the value of reserved seats is that they give women a chance to gain the experience of holding office in the Union, and of becoming known for their policies; without the reserved seats women have no chance, because members vote for the candidates they have heard of. Once women have gained this experience and prominence, they

100

should move on and give other women the chance, thus steadily increasing the number of experienced women trade unionists.

This proposal was not accepted by NUPE, but it raises interesting issues about the function of reserved seats. There are various perceptions of this function: either it is to ensure that women's issues are discussed at the highest level of the Union; or to affect national Union policy; or, through the authority of the Executive Councils, to affect policy at all levels of the Union; or to encourage greater participation by women members; or to give women experience of Trade Union organisation; or to deceive women members into believing that their interests are properly represented; or to silence women activists — or combinations of these. Although women trade unionists hold a wide range of views, it is agreed almost unanimously that reserved seats in themselves are not enough. The argument is over strategies, rather than objectives; it hinges on whether change should come first on policy issues or in trade union structures, and on whether structures should be changed from the top down or from the bottom up. There is also debate about whether having reserved seats results in a marginalising of women's issues.

Strategies for Change

Women in NALGO have chosen to concentrate on grassroots campaigning, and on policy matters before organisational issues. They argue that the increased involvement of women in the Union results from its prominent campaigning on women's issues, rather than from greater representation at Executive level, or even organisational changes at branch level. Women are often interested in becoming shop stewards, in order to do a job on behalf of the members they know in an area with which they are familiar; but beyond that they can be put off by the vast selection of meetings and committees and other activities. Also, because of their more chequered working lives, women are not likely to hold Trade Union offices for as long as men. There are increasing moves in NALGO toward enabling officials to job-share their posts.

The National Equal Opportunities Committee

Much emphasis in NALGO has been placed on informal methods of organising, and on workers' groups rather than committees. There is no national women's officer, although there is a research officer with responsibility for equal opportunities for women. In 1977 the Union set up a national Equal Opportunites Committee, which is responsible for work on women's rights and lesbian and gay rights. It has produced an impressive array of women's rights publications, and its work on issues such as sexual harassment has been in the forefront of trade union campaigning.

Black NALGO Members

NALGO policy on Black members is different from its policy on women, reflecting the very different problems Black men and women face and the much smaller presence of Black workers in NALGO's membership. NALGO supports the setting up of Black members' groups at branch, district and national level to ensure that the Union is capable of responding to their specific demands. Existing policy is in favour of a reserved seat for the chair of any national structure aimed a combatting racism.

Negotiating Priorities for Women in NALGO

NALGO has long supported policies on parental leave, improved maternity rights and anti-racism. In negotiations, it has increasingly been presented with attempts by management in local government to institute equal opportunities programmes, and in some instances has had to fight to ensure that the Union was involved in developing these programmes.

NALGO argues that these agreements cannot be sustained unless they are negotiated through the Union. According to the Union, experience has shown that most local authorities introduce policies which would have little impact on the inequalities that exist: Union involvement is necessary, therefore, to improve the proposals. Where the authority *is* pressing for strong policies, failure to recognise the crucial role of the Union in winning the support of the workforce can result in the failure of the policies. A positive action programme on recruitment which has not been properly negotiated also places an unfair burder on the new recruits, because they will be blamed for the inevitable conflict. This guarantees the failure of any anti-sexist or anti-racist policy: workplace practices cannot be changed simply by swelling the workforce with new recruits, and hoping that their input or even their mere presence will change attitudes.

Recently a lot of work has been done on campaigns for workplace nurseries, and negotiating time off for sick children. In 1986 a model equal opportunities agreement was produced at national level as a basis for negotiations.

NALGO's National Services and Conditions negotiating committee holds 'strategic discussion weekends', which include an equal opportunities component. There is no policy to ensure that officers with responsibility for equal opportunities should be involved in all negotiations, but the National Equal Opportunities Committee meets every 6 months with the chairs of all the negotiating committees to discuss priorities.

Conflicts for Trade Unionists

In devising policies on equal opportunities, particularly those which establish union procedures for tackling racial and sexual harassment at work, NALGO has brought to light the complexities for trade unionists in attempting to intervene in disputes between members, or to represent conflicting interests. This has also proved a thorny issue for other trade unionists. Where a union member accuses another member of sexual or racial harassment, the Union may find itself representing both sides to management: if it chooses between the two members, it will find itself performing a management function, co-operating with management in disciplining a member, and as such failing to provide its members with the promised support that Trade Unions can give. However, if it does not operate a policy on harassment, the Union is failing to represent the interests of its women and ethnic minority members.

NALGO is currently formulating policy to tackle this conflict. One option may be to provide members accused of harassment with observers at any disciplinary hearing in order to safeguard their rights; but to go no further than that. Meanwhile, the Union provides information, advice and representation to members who have been harassed, and it publicises its work on this as widely as possible.

Complexities also arise in negotiations for redundancy. For example, it is hard for the Union to argue for an alternative to redundancy based on natural wastage, although, as women leave their jobs to have children, this may well mean that more women are made redundant. In this situation the Union can work to protect and improve maternity leave agreements so that women who want to return to their jobs can do so more readily.

Another issue for NALGO has been whether jobs should be advertised internally before they are publicised generally. The Union acknowledges that internal advertising can be discriminatory in an unrepresentative workplace, but argues that its first responsibility is to protect the interests of its existing members.

Summary

The initiatives taken by Trade Unions on women's rights are clearly determined by the size of the Union, the proportion of women members, and the industries in which the Union is organised. Policies which are appropriate — or, indeed, possible — in one Union may not be in another. However, a few general features do emerge from steps taken by particular Trade Unions.

Firstly, it is very important for the Union to conduct a survey of its membership, to find out who it is representing and how well. A survey should help ascertain the position of women and ethnic minorities in the Union within different trade groups.

Secondly, the Union should identify the reasons for any under-representation the survey finds. These vary considerably from one workplace to another, and Union policies which ignore them will not work. They may include Union structures, lack of childcare provision, inaccessible times and locations of meetings and courses, intimidating procedures, hostility from male trade unionists, and the difficulty of organising in small or scattered workplaces.

Thirdly, the Union should decide on the measures necessary to increase women's involvement, and establish a procedure for implementing them. These measures should be monitored by committees or groups with sufficient authority to ensure that they are effective.

Finally, the Union should ensure that their enquiries and their recommendations are publicised widely throughout the Union; that there are opportunities for consultation with the membership; and that women members are encouraged to take part in, and advise on, all stages of a positive action programme in the Union.

The American Experience

We can learn from efforts which have been made in the United States to eradicate race and sex discrimination. However, there are certain differences which must be borne in mind, when considering how the US experience might be applied to the UK.

1. Pressure on the government

Legal measures to encourage and enforce affirmative action were largely a result of pressure put on the government by the civil rights movement, which aimed to improve the position of black people and other ethnic minorities. There was a genuine fear that there would be widespread civil disturbance if steps were not taken which, at least, appeared to meet some of demands of civil rights campaigners. This helped women improve their position in two ways: first, a strong women's movement emerged in the late 1960s which was inspired by, and benefitted from the experience of, the civil rights movement; and, second, laws designed to help ethnic minorities could be adapted to apply to women too. The UK has no equivalent history of a powerful civil rights movement.

2. Weaker Trade Unions

The US Trade Union movement has a very different role from its UK counterpart. A much smaller proportion of the workforce is unionised and the unions themselves are more heavily restricted by the law. Some sectors of employment, such as office work and nursing are largely unorganised and union-busting is more overt and respectable than in the UK.

As a result, employment legislation goes unenforced in many workplaces and relatively few workers are covered by collective agreements. On the other hand, individual workers are more inclined to take court action to solve employment problems, since they are less likely to be able to look to their unions for help. This contrasts with the UK, where major gains have been won by means of collective union action.

Studies in the US have also shown that a company's performance on affirmative action is not noticeably better where the company is unionised.

3. 'Class Actions'

The legal system in the US allows a case against an employer to be brought on behalf of a group of employees — several thousand is not an unusual number — all of whom may benefit if the action is successful. Clearly, this makes the law a more powerful weapon for promoting equality at work than it can be as it presently stands in the UK. In the UK, only the complainant benefits from a successful action, even if there are thousands of other people in exactly the same situation in a particular company.

The US Laws

Three pieces of legislation provide the framework for affiirmative action in the United States: the *1963 Equal Pay Act*; the *1964 Civil Rights Act* and the *1972 Equal Employment Opportunity Act*. These are broadly equivalent to Britain's *Equal Pay Act*, *Sex Discrimination Act* and *Race Relations Act*. The main differences for the purpose of this discussion, are that race and sex discrimination are dealt with by the same legislation; and the Equal Employment Opportunity Commission, an approximate equivalent of our EOC and Commission for Racial Equality, has power to take a case to court on behalf of an individual or group of individuals. In the UK, an individual complainant may get legal and financial assistance from the EOC or CRE, but she or he must formally initiate the action.

Contracts Compliance in the US

Although a ban on employment discrimination on grounds of race was imposed as a condition of government contracts during the Second World War, it was not until the early 1960s that the non-discrimination legislation was enacted.

1. In 1965, President Johnson issued an executive order (No. 11246) which for the first time made affirmative action measures compulsory. The Order forbade all government departments and all those employers who had contracts with the government worth more than $50,000 from discriminating against ethnic minorities. The Office of Federal Contract Compliance

(OFCCP) was set up to monitor the non-discrimination clauses in federal contracts.

2. In 1968, this was amended by Order 11375 to include discrimination on grounds of sex. The potential was enormous. There were estimated to be something like 40 million people or 40% of the national workforce working for government contractors. The orders covered not only contractors but sub-contractors and even establishments run by contractors which were connected with the particular government contract. This totals 300,000 companies, doing 100 billion dollars worth of business with the government.

3. In 1970 and 1971, two further Orders spelled out in detail exactly what employers had to do to comply with the original Order. This can be summarised as follows:

All contracts must include a non-discrimination clause — that is, a statement of intent not to discriminate; in addition, employers with more than 50 employees must:

a. Analyse their workforce by race and sex, and each year provide these details to the Office of Federal Contract Compliance.

b. Analyse major job classifications within their organisation and compare the numbers of women and minorities employed in them with the local labour pool.

c If the figures compare unfavourably (that is, the organisation employs smaller proportions of women and minorities than are available in the local labour pool) then the employer has to draw up an affirmative action plan to correct the deficiencies. This plan must include:

  i. goals: specific numbers of women and minorities to be employed in specific categories of jobs; and

  ii. timetables: specific dates by which the goals should be achieved.

d. All internal and external policy statements issued by the employer must declare a commitment to Equal Employment Opportunity.

e. An executive must be appointed to supervise the affirmative action effort.

4. The EEOC issued guidelines for achieving goals and timetables, which include:

a. Have the personnel manager speak at schools which minority and female students attend.

b. Run active recruitment at schools with predominantly female and minority enrolment.

c. Add minority and female placement and recruiting sources, such as Women's Employment Projects, to those already used.

d. Advertise in minority newspapers, women's journals, and on foreign language broadcasts.

e. Publicise female promotions in local press and women's interest media.

f. Hold briefing sessions and provide tour facilities for minority and female organisations.

g. Encourage minority and female employees to introduce, from among their acquaintances, applicants for vacancies.

h. Analyse job descriptions to ensure that they reflect the functions of the jobs, and do not simply describe the current (male) job holder.

i. Review job qualifications to ensure that they do not have a discriminatory effect and that they are absolutely necessary for the job.

j. Review selection processes, including testing, to eliminate bias.

k. Train management and personnel employees in how to put an affirmative action programme into practice.

l. Form an Equal Employment Opportunity Committee which includes representatives of all employees.

m. Set up a skill inventory system to identify promotable minority and female employees.

n. Set up formal reporting system to monitor applications, transfers, promotions and employees who leave.

By following these guidelines, employers can show that a 'good faith effort' is being made to implement the affirmative action programme, even if they fail to achieve their specified goals. It is necessary to convince the OFCCP that they have either achieved their goals within set timetables, or are making a good faith effort to do so. Failure on both counts could, theoretically, lead to the contract being withdrawn — a powerful sanction. *It is important to remember that the employers set their own goals, not the government.*

The concept of 'good faith' effort is important because it means the employer need not fear losing the contract by not imposing strict quotas on hirings and promotions in order to meet the affirmative action goals. Thus if the employer can demonstrate 'good faith' considerable flexibility is still possible.

The purpose in setting goals and timetables is to ensure that a real, measurable effort is made to encourage people with appropriate qualifications to apply for jobs on a non-discriminatory basis, and to correct the effects of past discrimination on current workforce patterns.

In developing goals for women and ethnic minorities the OFCCP requires employers to look at population, local unemployment, the local labour force, skill levels, recruitment possibilities, availability of training externally, promotion potential of existing employees and training availability within the company. The results of this analysis should produce a realistic figure for the employment of women and minorities.

Once set, a timescale for achieving the goals is agreed with the OFCCP. Order 11246, which concerns contractors dealing with the Federal Government, is monitored by 1,000 employees of the OFCCP across the USA. The ultimate sanction is the same as for contract compliance in the UK — that the contractor who does not try to achieve equality of opportunity may *be debarred from tendering for contract or can be investigated by the OFCCP.*

The national regulations are mirrored at City and State levels by local legislation imposing affirmative action as a condition of contracting with public authorities. In the case of some cities, the local legislation may include discrimination on the grounds of sexual orientation, or require special efforts to recruit locally based women or ethnic minorities. *Additionally, from among the approved contractors, the city may positively attempt to award contracts to women or minority owned businesses* where it appears there have been, in the past, few of them receiving public contracts.

Other Employing Organisations Where Affirmative Action Programmes can be Introduced

The *Civil Rights Act of 1964* says the courts can impose affirmative action programmes as a requirement to remedy sex and race discrimination. Therefore, if a complaint of sex or race discrimination is made against an employer — whether the employer holds a contract with the government or not — and the complaint is upheld, an affirmative action programme could be introduced as part of the settlement imposed by the Court.

Furthermore, the *1972 Equal Employment Act* empowered the EEOC to include an affirmative action programme in any agreement reached through conciliation; that is as part of a negotiated settlement agreed before the trial. Most of the affirmative action programmes in America have been introduced by this method and rarely incorporate an admission of past discrimination. Therefore, in the eyes of the law, there is no proof of past discrimination.

The Difference Between 'Quotas' and 'Goals and Timetables'

On both sides of the Atlantic, much of the resistance to the idea of affirmative or positive action stems from a misunderstanding of the distinction between quotas and goals. Essentially, the difference is that neither the goal nor the time within which it is to be achieved is rigid: if the OFCCP is satisfied that a 'good faith effort' is being made to reach a goal, it will accept extensions to the timetable. Quota systems *are* rigid, and create manifold problems.

A strict quota system can result in reverse discrimination, which is extremely unpopular; and ultimately, it can also result in further discrimination against the very people it is supposed to advance. For instance, *before* a quota is met, employers will turn down suitable white male applicants because they are anxious to fill the quota first; and *after* the quota is met, they will resume their previous hiring practices, cease to concern themselves with under-representation — and able applicants from under-represented groups will again be discriminated against.

Thus, a quota system is an extremely unambitious method of countering inequalities. It introduces an unacceptable element of randomness into hiring procedures; it does not correct the underlying discrimination in these procedures; and it is used as a lazy, short-cut method towards combatting discrimination. Further problems arise where an employer introduces a 'double quota', in order to increase the numbers of two or more under-represented groups (for instance, Black people and women). Applicants who are members of both groups are likely to have a better chance of being accepted because the resulting overlap increases the size of both quotas.

Most importantly, quotas are not necessary. People who are employed under quota systems have their status as 'second class' employees underpinned; and the adoption of such a system confirms a management prejudice that under-represented groups can *only* progress if they are given unfair advantages. In reality, if hiring procedures and training facilities are improved, and realistic timetables set, and if discriminatory job requirements — such as an unnecessary insistence on seniority — are removed, employers can correct imbalances in the workforce without ever resorting to reverse discrimination.

The legality of quotas in the USA

Some affirmative action programmes in the US have involved

110

quotas — with the result that in some cases white males have gone to court claiming that they have suffered unlawful discrimination. Two important test cases went to the Supreme Court:

The Bakke Case

During the 1970s, as part of its affirmative action plan, the University of California Medical School decided to reserve 16% of its places for candidates from designated minority groups.

Alan Bakke, a white man, applied to the school in 1973 and 1974 and was turned down both times. In the same years, minority students with fewer qualifications than Bakke were admitted into the quota places. It should be remembered that all students had to prove themselves competent to study at the school; but less weight was put on academic qualifications in the case of minority students.

Bakke successfully sued the University for wrongful discrimination; and the Californian courts ordered the School to admit him. The School appealed to the Supreme Court, which agreed that Bakke should be given a place. However, the Supreme Court Justices could *not* reach agreement as to whether 'race-conscious programmes' to correct past discriminations were in general lawful and constitutional. They ruled against this particular programme, but said that race-conscious programmes *would* be lawful to remedy past discrimination if it had been identified by the government.

The Weber Case

In 1979 the Supreme Court returned to this issue when it considered the case of Kaiser Aluminium *v*. Weber. Kaiser had entered into a collective bargaining agreement with the union, the United Steelworkers of America, that 50% of new recruits would be from designated minority groups, and that 50% of in-plant craft training places would be allotted to minority applicants. This quota was designed to correct the virtual exclusion of minorities from craft jobs — a result of the requirement that in-plant trainees must have previous experience. Kaiser had embarked on this plan under government pressure.

Brian Weber, a white man, applied for training and was rejected. He then discovered that the two most junior minority trainees had less experience than several of the white workers who had been turned down. As only 13 training places were available, and Weber was only 44th in seniority of all applicants, he would not have been accepted even without the quota. However, he sued Kaiser under the Civil Rights Act on the grounds that it was illegal to use race rather than seniority as a basis for selection.

In deciding the case, the Supreme Court looked at the purpose of the legislation. This they found to be the elimination of discrimination in American society; they therefore refused to interpret the bar on discrimination in the Civil Rights Act as prohibiting race-conscious steps taken to eliminate 'manifest racial imbalances in traditionally segregated job categories.' They further found the Kaiser programme to be legal because it was a temporary measure, did not absolutely exclude white workers from training, and did not require the dismissal of any white employees. The Weber judgment also affirmed the principle laid down in the Bakke judgment: that quotas *could* be used to further a 'compelling state interest' such as overcoming *government-identified* discrimination.

Some Examples of Affirmative Action

The Bank of America

The Bank of America provides an interesting example of what affirmative action can achieve in as little as five years.

The Class Action Against the Bank

In 1971 the Bank was sued by three international division employees, who alleged sex discrimination in hiring, training opportunities, and promotions. They were joined in the action by the EEOC who had by this time the power to take court action. The women took action on behalf of themselves and also of a 'class' comprising 'all past and present women employees and applicants for employment of the Bank and its subsidiaries'. It was estimated that this class included a possible 64,000 claimants.

The case never reached the courts because the Bank agreed to a settlement, eventually approved by the court in the form of a 'consent decree'.

The Affirmative Action Programme

The decree was to run for five years and was subject to monitoring by the plaintiff's lawyers and the courts. It included:
- back pay awards;
- the setting up of four trust funds to train women for promotion;
- the setting of goals for the promotion of women within the Bank, to be achieved within five years;
- the promotion of opportunities to take up to one year's leave of absence to pursue non-vocational interests, for women who would no longer benefit from the Bank's management training.

Results

The Bank exceeded its overall goals, and by 1978, 54% of its officer grades were filled by women. These were mostly in junior and middle management grades, however: only 40 women had achieved top managerial posts, although this compared with five women in 1972.

It was later discovered that the Bank was still favouring senior male executives by paying for their membership of exclusive male-only clubs; thus, not only were women barred from what was undoubtedly an informal network for promotions, but the Bank was subsidising their exclusion. Only when the US Treasury threatened to withdraw its contract did the Bank discontinue this practice. Nonetheless, the programme did enable several thousand women to progress to middle management levels: they would not otherwise have been promoted.

AT & T

The American Telephone and Telegraph Company is the world's largest corporation. In 1979 it declared a profit of £2.85 billion after tax.

The Consent Decree

The EEOC, prompted by over 2,000 complaints, joined together with women's and minority pressure groups in 1970 to take action against this corporate giant. Discrimination at every stage of employment was alleged. AT & T denied the charges and it took until 1973 to negotiate the settlement.

Analysis of AT & T's workforce showed that there was extensive job segregation: 92.4% of the workforce of 980,000 worked in jobs with at least 90% of one sex in them. Further, salary increases on promotion were based on the old salary rather than the new job. The resulting disparity in pay penalised women in particular, because they were starting out in lower paid jobs.

The Affirmative Action Programme

The 1973 court decree instructed AT & T to compensate employees for discriminatory wage rates, and to give them parity. Altogether the company was committed to paying £50 million in back pay to women and minority employees. It was also committed to a 5-year plan for the hiring, training and promotion of women and minorities. A long-term goal of 38% women employees in all job categories was set. However, it was recognised that external factors —

such as women's disproportionate family responsibilities — contributed to their unavailability for work, so the court set intermediate goals, to be reached within 6 years. Goals for the hiring of women in non-traditional areas were set artificially high, in anticipation of a high drop-out rate. Goals were also set for recruiting men into the secretarial and administrative jobs traditionally done by women.

The company also undertook to rewrite all job descriptions and advertisements, to use female recruiting staff, and to adapt and redesign technical equipment so that women could use it. Members of staff were given special training to explain the programme, and managers were assessed annually on their 'equal opportunity performance.'

It was discovered that, although 34% of workers in management grades were women, these grades included secretarial staff, of whom 94% were women. Women were very poorly represented in middle to upper management grades. Women who had entered AT & T as graduates and had not been offered any management training were to be assessed for promotion and compensated with back pay.

As an indication of the scale on which AT & T was operating, during the first five years of the decree there were approximately 500,000 openings for new jobs or promotions. As a result of the decree, almost half of these went to women and minorities.

The Affirmative Action Override

The goals set for AT & T were not fixed quotas, but when, after the first years of the decree, the company had only achieved half of them, it was taken back to court. Its failure was largely attributable to the refusal of the union, the Communication Workers of America (CWA), to contemplate any promotion system not based on strict seniority.

The court established an agreement, known as the 'affirmative action override', whereby adequately-qualified women and minority candidates for promotion were to be given preference over more senior white males. This was seen as a temporary but necessary expedient, and withstood a challenge from the CWA in the courts. The override was lifted as soon as 90% of the goal was reached in each job category.

Results

A general co-ordinating committee, involving AT & T management and government enforcement agencies, monitored the AT & T programme. In 1978 the corporation's senior management acknowledged that the programme would have had little impact without this monitoring and the government compulsion.

In 1972 women had occupied 2.1% of the middle to upper management positions: by 1978 this had increased to 6.7%. This was more than double the proportion of women in comparable jobs in other corporations. In the outside craft jobs women progressed from 0.2% of the total to 2.8%: in the inside craft grades their participation increased from 6% to 14% of the total. After a poor start and a return to court, by 1978 AT & T had achieved 99% of its overall targets.

Greyhound Bus Company

Greyhound Bus Company imposed a minimum height requirement of 5′ 7″ for all bus drivers. A class action was taken against it alleging that this requirement discriminated against women and was unnecessary. The case was settled out of court.

The Affirmative Action Programme

The company agreed to take steps to recruit and train women drivers until their numbers reflected their availability in the labour pool. Until this goal was achieved the company agreed to reserve 25% of the places at its Driver Training School for women. Changes in recruiting methods were agreed in anticipation of problems filling these places: the height requirement was dropped; advertising and promotional literature was to depict women and to state clearly that previous bus driving experience was not necessary; and women's magazines and women's organisations were to be added to the company's publicity lists. Very detailed provisions about advertising were negotiated so that the company could not claim that women were simply not interested in the work.

Other measures in the Greyhound agreement included giving all women trainees who failed their assessment a second chance; holding annual seminars for recruitment and training staff and evaluating their work, and monitoring and adjusting the programme at regular intervals.

What Effect has Affirmative Action had on Women's Jobs Generally?

It is important to remember that there has only been a decade and a half of affirmative action with goals and timetables for hiring and

115

promoting women. Therefore no dramatic changes can reasonably be expected at the top of any job category, because women who have been hired or promoted have not yet had time to accumulate the necessary experience to proceed to the top.

It is widely acknowledged that publicity given to the AT & T settlement encouraged other large corporations who are concerned about their public image to take the equality legislation seriously. Many of them have begun affirmative action programmes on a voluntary basis in order to avoid court action or the threat of sanctions from the government in the form of lost contracts.

However, by 1985, figures indicated that, on average, companies were achieving only 10% of their goals. This held true at whatever level the goals were set. All well as showing that companies are anxious not to be *too* successful with their equal opportunities programmes, this also provides a strong argument for setting the goals artificially high.

In the manual trades, particularly construction and mining, affirmative action in training by women's organisations and public training agencies have resulted in a slow but real increase in women entering these non-traditional and better paid-occupations. In the construction industry, union membership is a prerequisite for obtaining apprenticeships or employment. In 1970, 0.6% of the union membership and 6.5% of the craft labour force was female. *By 1976, the figure had risen to 1.6% of the union membership and 8.5% of the craft labour force.*

There is no equivalent in the USA of the UK's protective legislation preventing women from entering the coal mining industry, although historically this highly-paid occupation had a 100% male workforce. In 1970 there were no women in coal mines. Using their rights to equal employment opportunity under the 1964 legislation, women began to apply for jobs, and by 1980 there were 3,295 female coal miners, representing 8.7% of the workforce.

On the other hand, general statistics still look bleak. Women make up 42% of the US workforce, yet 33 million of them (80% of all women workers) are in clerical, service, sales, factory or plant jobs. This is a slight improvement on the position twenty years ago and roughly equivalent to the improvement in the UK.

As for pay, nationally women earn 62% of what men earn, compared with 60% in 1972. Women in management earn only 60% of their male counterparts, while women in technical and professional occupations are a little better — taking home 70% of the earnings of their male equivalents.

While these figures cannot detract from the very real benefits which have occured to women directly affected by affirmative action programmes, they indicate the limitations of affirmative action as a device for promoting equality in terms of pay. These are partly due to inherent weaknesses in some affirmative action programmes, and partly due to other factors. For example:

1. *'Category inflation'*

Some companies try to convey the impression that they have increased the numbers of women in non-traditional areas, including managerial grades, simply by re-defining jobs. For example, a company may re-name a secretarial job an 'executive post' without any change in the salary or the work itself.

2. *Limited scope of some programmes*

Programmes are ineffective unless they tackle the job segregation which perpetuates low pay for women. For example, the City College of New York has substantially increased its female faculty members to a total of 25%. A closer look, however, reveals that the nursing department is nearly 100% female, while the science department is nearly all male.

3. *Part-time workers*

A great many women hold part-time jobs and — as in the UK — part-time workers have inferior rights. Their status under affirmative action programmes has not yet been clearly defined, so many are unable to benefit from them.

4. *More progress by minority men than by women*

Studies undertaken by the OFCCP and by Doctor Jonathan Leonard of the University of California indicate that minority men have achieved more than women in getting into jobs normally held by white men. In addition, their earnings have increased from 59% of white men's earnings in 1965, to 71% in 1978; whilst women's earnings as a whole were still only 62% of men's in 1985.

The progress made by minority men is valuable in itself; but affirmative action programmes need to have safeguards built in to ensure that employers eliminate *all* aspects of discrimination in hiring practice and salary scales. Partial efforts are insufficient, and any partial approach will inevitably exclude women from minority groups.

Studies on the effectiveness of Affirmative Action

1. *The OFCCP*

In 1983 the OFCCP itself carried out a review of 77,000 companies employing 20 million employees over the period 1974–80. A comparison was made between companies who were obliged to undertake affirmative action as federal contractors, and companies who were not.

The results of the survey showed clearly that women and ethnic minorities made significantly greater gains both as a proportion of the total workforce, and in terms of their relative status within it in companies contracting with the government.

Between 1974–80, the number of minority employees in companies contracting with the government increased by 20% compared to only a 12% increase for minorities in companies not contracting with the government. *For women the figure was 15% as opposed to 2%.*

2. *Dr Leonard's study*

This study, *The Impact of Affirmative Action* (National Bureau of Economic Research, 1983), surveyed approximately 17,000 companies who were Federal contractors and thus obliged to undertake affirmative action. His findings broadly paralleled those of the OFCCP's study. He also indicated that the employment gains made by disadvantaged groups were not temporary: whilst the employment of women and ethnic minorities increased at a faster rate in plants where the workforce was expanding, those where the workforce was static or contracting were not losing higher proportions of female and minority employees. The study also compared affirmative action under Federal contract compliance with that imposed on companies by the Court as a result of a class action case. He examined 1,700 cases taken under the Civil Rights Act and found that class actions had a relatively stronger impact on individual plants, but that fewer employees and plants were affected by the individual cases.

The future

Currently, there is a dispute within the Reagan administration as to whether affirmative action is effective, whether it hampers business, and whether the provisions of Order 11246 should be diluted.

Organisations representing business interests do not necessarily oppose affirmative action. In November 1985, the National Association of Manufacturers wrote to President Reagan on behalf of their 13,500 members asking for the retention of Order 11246 as it is. Futhermore, a 1984 study by *Organisation Resources Counsellors* indicated that out of 215 of the largest corporations in the USA 95% planned to continue their affirmative action programmes with goals and timetables regardless of any change in Order 11246. This would help them avoid disruption and expense if the Order were subsequently reinstated; but many corporations have noted the considerable advantages to themselves in affirmative action.

Summary of lessons which can be learned from the US experience

1. It is vital to compile accurate data about the actual potential workforce, if realistic goals are to be set for the utilisation of women.
2. Affirmative action programmes must be drawn up in considerable detail if they are to have any impact.
3. Possible avoidance tactics by the employer must be anticipated and guarded against.
4. It is important, too, to anticipate a high drop-out rate among women affected by affirmative action measures. The reasons (e.g. women's family commitments) must be understood and steps taken to compensate for the drop-out rate by a higher initial intake.
5. It is essential to collect sufficient data and establish effective machinery to monitor the progress of an affirmative action programme.
6. If an affirmative action programme is taken seriously by a company, all employees involved in personnel work must be committed to its goals — and trained to implement them properly.
7. Publicity given to affirmative action programmes can have a useful spin-off effect, especially when affirmative action comes to be regarded as a good employment practice.
8. Affirmative action in employment and training cannot alone bring about equality. The need for fundamental changes in other areas too — not least in education, and in the policies of Trade Unions — must not be overlooked.
9. In times of economic recession, affirmative action can be applied to redundancy agreements so that women do not suffer more than men, where the 'last in, first out' rule would normally apply.

119

Making the Law More Effective

As we pointed out at the beginning of this book, the equality legislation has not substantially improved the position of women at work: women are still largely confined to low-paid, low status, dead-end jobs. The laws are ineffective without positive action to tackle both job segregation, and traditional, discriminatory evaluations of the worth of women's work. However, there is also an urgent need for changes in public policy, particularly in the area of education and training, and there is a need for changes in the laws themselves, in how they are interpreted, and in how they are administered. This section looks at the role of education and training in determining women's job opportunities, and discusses a number of proposals for strengthening the Sex Discrimination and Equal Pay Acts.

Education and Training

The Sex Discrimination Act outlaws discrimination in the provision of education and training as well as in employment, although these sections of the legislation are very little used. There is a great volume of evidence to show that sex-stereotyping begins even before children reach school age – and that it is compounded and strengthened throughout the educational process. There is a tendency for both educators and employers to blame one another for this sex-differentiation: employers, on the one hand, argue that they cannot hire more young women because their qualifications are inadequate or inappropriate for the jobs available; and teachers respond that young women do not acquire the necessary skills because employers still do not hire them. Since the early 1980s there has been a growing emphasis on vocational training for young people, and a resultant increase in employer-led training. In this context it is clear that neither employers nor educators can abdicate responsibility for the persistence with which young women are funnelled toward a restricted range of training and jobs.

1. Schools

There is much detailed information available showing how sex segregation in education develops and leads into eventual sex segregation in employment. Children start school with generally similar skills and abilities, but by the time they reach secondary schools and start entering public examinations, there are striking sex differences, with fewer girls learning scientific and technical subjects, and an overall underachievement amongst girls. Women are also under-represented amongst teaching staff, particularly in more senior posts.

We do not intend, here, to outline a detailed programme for positive action in education. However, the Equal Opportunities Unit of the Inner London Education Authority provides an interesting example of how institutional sex discrimination in schools can be tackled:

In 1979, in a mixed secondary school in London, only one girl had enrolled for 'O' level physics. The science staff therefore decided to use a female physics teacher; to include in the course a section on the social relevance of physics; to explain opportunities in physics more fully to 3rd-year girls; to discredit the myth of physics being a male subject; and to ask older physics students in the school to promote the subject at option time. Two years later, in 1981, there were 28 girls on the 'O' level physics course. [See ILEA: *Race, Sex and Class —achievement in schools* 1983.]

2. Youth training

The government's Youth Training Scheme provides the bulk of youth training in the UK. Overall, the YTS is managed by the Manpower Services Commission (MSC), and as such reflects the MSC's philosophy on equal opportunities. Thus, although the YTS has a policy on equal access to all training, and although some of the MSC's minuscule 'special needs' budget for women is funnelled towards training for young women, the MSC is not prepared to develop a national positive action programme.

Young women are under-represented on the YTS, making up 44% of trainees. In some areas of training, such as information technology, this figure falls as low as 20%. A 1984 report, *The Class of 84*, produced jointly by the Fawcett Society and the National Joint Committee of Working Women's Organisations, found that sex-stereotyping was a major factor reducing young women's access to the high level skills training available to some YTS trainees. Many of the young women interviewed for the report

121

had been directed away from 'unsuitable' or 'unfeminine' courses of training. Thus, the 'job-related training' available on the YTS continues to channel women into traditional, low-paid jobs and industries.

Furthermore, the MSC refuses to make any provision for childcare on its training schemes. This is, of course, a more significant barrier to women applying for places on adult training schemes; but in 1985 the Women in Youth Training Group estimated that this policy would affect a minimum of 5% of women entering the YTS.

3. Post-school education

Men outnumber women in almost every area of further and higher education. Although the proportion of women undertaking courses of post-school education is increasing rapidly, they are still massively under-represented in all but the most traditional subjects, such as language and literature studies; courses in social work, nursing and nursery nursing; and clerical and secretarial courses. However, recent years have seen an increasing recognition of the need for greater flexibility in the provision of post-school education. The supposition that students will enrol directly from school has, in particular, resulted in indirect sex discrimination, as women are much less likely to conform to this pattern. A number of further education colleges, polytechnics and universities now offer returner courses — variously known as 'Fresh Start', 'Wider Opportunities for Women', 'New Horizons' and 'Return to Work' — which are designed to help women equip themselves with work-related skills.

4. Employer-based training

Fewer women enter jobs which involve long periods of training; a high proportion of women work part-time, and are therefore automatically refused training by many employers; fewer women are recruited into the grades which carry training opportunities; and a much smaller proportion of female than male employees gets offered the chance of skills training to improve promotion prospects. For example, male workers are four times as likely to obtain day or block release from work in order to train externally for work-related qualifications. Training opportunities at work should be included in any positive action programme (see p. 57) but it is important not to overlook youth training, apprenticeships, and recruitment training of every kind in such a programme.

5. Adult Training

As with the YTS, the MSC has the primary responsibility for government-funded adult training, and its influence extends to the training proffered by local education authorities.

Unfortunately, as we have indicated, the MSC tends to regard women as a special, minority category of trainees. Its 'special needs' budget is intended to cater not just for women, but also for ethnic minorities, ex-prisoners, people with disabilities, and ex-forces personnel; and the money available for all of this is less than 1% of the MSC's annual budget.

Some useful initiatives in women's training have been taken within this 'special needs' formula; and the MSC has tried experimental training schemes, some of them specifically for women, in order to expand women's job opportunities across a wider range of industries, occupations and skills. However, its national priorities remain to improve all training opportunities and, rather than adopting positive action measures, to continue to provide 'equal access' for all. In the context of pervasive sex discrimination, this policy merely reinforces a discriminatory status quo.

Many of the obstacles encountered by women in acquiring education and training are similar to those in employment, and they are similarly worsened in economic recession. Women have patchy training histories for the same reasons as they have chequered working lives, and they have similar requirements for childcare, flexible hours, maternity rights and facilities for part-timers. School students conform, both in subject choices and in career plans, to outdated sex role stereotypes, and many female school leavers have very low expectations of work and little interest in further training. However, the number of women seeking opportunities in adult training indicates that these expectations change very rapidly. Women are then at a disadvantage because training strategies are primarily geared to the male pattern of continuous training followed by continuous employment. In recent years, some employers and Trade Unions — chiefly in the public sector — have negotiated changes in eligibility and age requirements for apprentices and other trainees, in order to counter this indirect discrimination. However, a recognition of women's particular training and educational requirements has yet to be incorporated into national training policy: nor have there been sufficient efforts by training bodies and educational institutions to apply positive action measures to all their courses and facilities. In 1984 the government issued a white paper, *Training for Jobs*, which dealt in detail with government proposals for improving education and training across

123

the board. In contrast with previous government documents about these issues, the white paper made *no* specific reference to training for women. There is thus every indication that women's training needs have again become a low priority issue for Central Government.

Legislating for Change

As we explained earlier, sections 47 and 48 of the Sex Discrimination Act affirm that it is *not unlawful* for training bodies and employers, under certain circumstances, to provide special training for women. Any other form of exclusive provision is unlawful.

This is the only reference to positive action in the Sex Discrimination legislation. It is inadequate in itself, and we suggest possible improvements below. However, the existence of these sections indirectly creates two additional difficulties. Firstly, they have been widely interpreted to mean that no other form of positive action is lawful: in other words, that if the legislation does not specifically permit something, it is unlawful. The inaction of some employers and trade unionists on sex equality — and, similarly, on race equality — can in part be attributed to this. Secondly, these forms of positive action are *optional*, and as a result very few employers have troubled to find out about them, let alone introduce them. If positive action is to be developed on a wide scale throughout industry and the public services, and if reluctant employers (and, indeed, reluctant unions or employees) are to be persuaded to accept such programmes, legal backing will be required. In other words, it will be necessary to enforce a duty on employers to examine the needs of their workforce, to set goals and timetables, and to report on progress.

Proposals of this kind are greeted with outrage by many employers and legislators, on the basis that they would contravene an unwritten philosophy that everyone should be treated equally by the law. In fact, of course, the Disabled Persons' (Employment) Act 1944 already goes much further than this: rather than simply imposing a requirement to consider positive measures, it obliges employers of more than 20 people to employ a 3% *quota* of registered disabled persons (see p. 7).

Section 71 of the Race Relations Act 1976

The Race Relations Act 1976 also provides a context for legislation for positive action. S.71 places a duty on local authorities to ensure that they carry out all of their functions with regard to the need to promote equality of opportunity, to eliminate unlawful racial discrimination, and to promote good race relations.

We believe that this part of the Race Relations Act is equally necessary in the Sex Discrimination Act, but also that it needs to be improved upon. S.71 has been applied by some local authorities specifically to their employment practices (see p. 6) but its wording is so imprecise that any steps taken under it are, in effect, optional. As with the *intentionally* optional provisions for positive action in the Sex Discrimination Act, the result of this is to persuade local authorities that measures not fully spelt out in the statutes are unnecessary, or actually unlawful. Again, many local authorities have thereby been inhibited from doing anything at all. Further, as we have pointed out, there are no guidelines for interpreting this part of the legislation.

NCCL therefore proposes the following additions to s.71:

Firstly, of course, it should be extended in full to the Sex Discrimination Act, so that corresponding provisions exist for countering both sex and race discrimination.

Secondly, the responsibilities outlined should not be confined to local authorities, but should be extended to all public and publicly-funded bodies. This would mean that all public sector employers, all tiers of government, and all providers of public services and utilities, would be bound by the same statutory duties.

Thirdly, these duties should be spelt out clearly. Public bodies should be required to examine both their employment practices and their provision of services to ensure that they are not discriminating, either directly or indirectly. The legislation should specify areas which might merit a closer look (such as childcare provision, the status and entitlements of part-time workers, and the use of interpreters and translators in public communications) and guidelines should be issued explaining possible remedies. Without these, the provision is unenforceable.

Finally, public bodies should be required to publish regular reports of the work they are doing to fulfill their obligations in promoting equal opportunities. As well as ensuring public accountability, this could generate valuable discussion about how best to bring about change.

125

Contracts Compliance

Another way to provide a stronger legal framework for positive action would be to bring contracts compliance more fully into the scope of the law. At present local authorities are *empowered* but not *obliged* to attach conditions relating to equal opportunities to their public contracts. Because only a few local authorities have chosen to do so, and because the measure only works if the contract is worth a lot of money, contracts compliance has so far been of limited value. However, it has enormous potential, as the US experience has shown. It is one obvious way of defining the responsibilities of local authorities under s.71 of the Race Relations Act. It is also a valuable means of transporting good practice from the public sector into the private sector.

What is necessary is to include a requirement in all government contracts, that the contractor put into effect a programme designed to break down job segregation and improve job prospects for women and ethnic minority workers. By 'government contracts' we mean those tendered by central government bodies as well as by local authorities, including health and education authorities and other statutory bodies. The requirement could take the form of a Positive Action Resolution, outlined below.

This would make it much more difficult for private employers to duck their responsibilities simply by finding new purchasers, and it would also lead to better employment practice by the public bodies issuing contracts. However, in order for it to work, it is necessary to specify very clearly what is being required of contractors, and what targets are being set. Otherwise there is a danger that they will ensure their eligibility to compete for contracts with a few cosmetic measures only.

In the current economic and political climate, it is often argued that the principles of the 'free market' should determine the allocation of contracts, and that open competition should not be impeded by equal opportunity considerations. We do not intend, here, to discuss general economic issues; but we disagree with this argument on two counts.

Firstly, we do not accept that any commercial considerations should be allowed to outweigh the principles underlying our legislation — in this instance, the equality legislation. They should most certainly not be given automatic precedence. Contracts compliance is a measure designed to ensure compliance with the letter and spirit of our law, not with some arbitrary, impractical standard of good practice. *Secondly*, we see no reason why a company's record on equal opportunities should not be perceived as a clear measure of its viability, and its suitability to undertake a job or service, in the same way that its financial records are examined. The chief resource that any contractor has to offer is its workforce, and an employer who takes equal opportunity issues seriously is likely to have good practices on recruitment, training, and industrial relations.

A Positive Action Resolution

The idea of including terms other than commercial ones in government contracts is not foreign to this country. Since 1946 the House of Commons 'Fair Wages Resolution' has required all employers tendering for government contracts to provide 'the recognised terms and conditions' of the industry for their employees. A Trade Union which believes that the recognised terms are not being met can take a complaint to the Central Arbitration Committee (CAC) on behalf of its members. In 1975, the Employment Protection Act extended this protection to all employees, whether or not they were working for a government contractor. Schedule 11 of the Act allowed a Union to apply to the CAC for improvements in pay or conditions if these were less favourable than those in the industry as a whole, or those generally provided in the area. However, Schedule 11 was repealed by the Employment Act 1980.

We would like to see the introduction of a 'Positive Action Resolution', corresponding to the Fair Wages Resolution, as a means of operating contracts compliance. The resolution would be included in all government contracts, and it would require the employer to negotiate, agree, and implement a positive action programme, which would involve analysing the workforce, identifying the jobs in which women and ethnic minority workers are under-represented, and drawing up a detailed programme to remedy the situation.

To ensure the effectiveness of the Resolution, progress would have to be closely monitored. We propose that the Equal Opportunities Commission and the Commission for Racial Equality should be responsible for ensuring that employers monitored progress. If an employer refuses to negotiate a positive action agreement, or if the agreement is inadequate or not being implemented, the EOC or the CRE should be able to apply to the CAC for a ruling directing the employer either to implement a programme or to modify the terms of an agreed programme. Similarly, a trade union should have the power to complain to the CAC if the employer refuses to act, as should an individual employee.

The Fair Wages Resolution does not apply to government departments themselves: presumably it is assumed that they will pay a 'fair rate' for the job as a result of collective bargaining. But it certainly cannot be assumed that government departments will voluntarily adopt positive action programmes. We therefore propose that the Positive Action resolution should apply to government departments as well as to government contractors.

Strengthening the Central Arbitration Committee

In addition to implementing the Fair Wages Resolution, the CAC is responsible under the Equal Pay Act for amending directly discriminatory pay structures — i.e. pay structures with different rates for men and women. Most such pay schemes had already been eliminated by 1975 when the Act came into force, but the CAC used its powers to amend a wide range of pay structures and agreements which were *indirectly* discriminatory, where the effect of the grading system was to keep women at the bottom. However, in 1979 the High Court ruled that the CAC had over-stepped its legal powers. The CAC had been asked by the union to consider a collective agreement at Hy-Mac Ltd. Although the agreement had been renegotiated after 1975, there were no women in the two highest paid grades and 70% of them were concentrated in the lowest grades. The CAC agreed that, although overt discrimination had been eliminated, the agreement still embodied the idea of a man's rate and a woman's rate for particular jobs. They devised a new pay structure. Hy-Mac appealed to the High Court, which ruled that the CAC were not entitled to carry out a general wages review, but could only amend the agreement by eliminating men's rates and women's rates.

Furthermore, it is proposed in the 1986 Sex Discrimination Bill to repeal this section of the Equal Pay Act altogether. The Bill, amongst other things, sets out to bring UK legislation in line with European Community law by voiding discriminatory terms in collective agreements: it is argued that this renders the CAC completely superfluous, because it cannot amend a term which is void.

However, we consider that the CAC's jurisdiction in this area is still very necessary. The Sex Discrimination Bill as at September 1986 does not provide any alternative machinery whereby collective agreements which are thought to contain discriminatory provisions may be referred to an authority for consideration, and duly declared void. It may also prove necessary to provide for agreements to be amended rather than altogether voided, in order to avoid uncertainty and confusion for management and employees alike. The CAC is a specialist body, with considerable expertise to assist in the task of arbitration and enforcement here. It would therefore be more appropriate to extend its powers to amend directly and indirectly discriminatory agreements and pay structures, rather than curtail it.

Class Actions

In the USA, another route to affirmative action programmes has been through the *class action*, a legal device unknown in this country. Under the class action, a case can be brought against an employer on behalf of thousands of 'existing, future and potential' employees. It is thus possible for the court to make an extremely wide-ranging order, directing the company to implement an affirmative action programme which will reduce the risk of discrimination against any present or future employee, compensate for the effects of past discrimination and reduce the disadvantaged status of present and future employees.

The legal system in the UK is based on a very different view of what it is possible and desirable for legal action to achieve. Roughly speaking, employment law here is designed to provide an *individual* employee with a remedy against a specific, proveable wrong — such as an unfair dismissal, or a refusal of employment on grounds of sex. A decision in one case may result in employers changing their job specifications or requirements; but this will only occur where it is obvious that the individual complainant was the victim of a general rule and that other people would be similarly affected if the rule itself were not changed. In other cases, a successful claim by one woman may be ignored by the employer after the individual woman herself has left that job. (For instance, in one firm investigated by the EOC, a woman's successful equal pay claim did not prevent the employer from reducing the pay rate again once she had left. The only remedy for the new employee is to bring a fresh equal pay claim.)

Unfortunately, the courts in this country have shown themselves extremely reluctant to 'burden' employers with the demands of sex discrimination law. They would undoubtedly be extremely hostile to a law which enabled them to reach a decision which could affect hundreds of employees, which could dramatically change the employer's practices, and which could be very expensive to implement. Faced with the choice, they would no doubt interpret their powers extremely narrowly.

Nonetheless, we believe that it will eventually prove necessary to introduce some version of class action to this country. Although we recognise the difficulty in applying legislation to 'potential or future' employees, the Sex Discrimination and Race Relations Acts already go some way towards providing legal remedies, under employment law, for people who have been unfairly refused employment. Moreover, although judges may be reluctant to make decisions on behalf of hypothetical people not named in the action, it would be comparatively easy for the courts or the Industrial Tribunals to consider a group of cases brought by a number of women together (i.e. by picking out one or two 'test cases', the results of which would determine the outcome of all the cases).

Section 48 of the Sex Discrimination Act

A further question, when considering the law as it affects positive action programmes, is the interpretation of the present sections on positive action. Section 48 of the Sex Discrimination Act allows an employer to:

— give women employees only (or men employees only) access to training facilities which would equip them for work which women have previously not done (or done only in small numbers); and
— encourage women only (or men only) to take advantage of opportunities for doing that kind of work.

No discrimination at the actual point of selection is permitted: in other words, the employer cannot take on a woman for non-traditional work simply because she is a woman. We are not suggesting that this be allowed or encouraged. The problem is that the existing provisions for positive training are limited to existing employees. Thus, it is possible for the employer to run women-only training courses to equip manual women workers for skilled work, or women secretaries to move into junior management. But it is not possible for the employer to put them on a special training course and then invite them to apply (on equal terms with other employees, both men and women) for permanent management posts. The Act needs to be amended to allow an employer to recruit women for special training courses, as well as providing such courses for existing employees.

Strengthening the Commissions

The EOC and the CRE have corresponding responsibilities: they were both given duties in their particular spheres to work towards eliminating discrimination and to promote equality of opportunity. They are at present the only bodies with a statutory public accountability for this work.

They were also both mandated to 'keep under review' the legislation which established them — in the CRE's case the Race Relations Act, and in the EOC's case both the Sex Discrimination and Equal Pay Acts. This monitoring role is open to various interpretations, but certainly the intention was that the *effectiveness* of the legislation should be kept under scrutiny; and that the Commissions, as experts in the field, should make recommendations for change wherever appropriate. This implies an original uncertainty on the part of our legislators as to the quality of the laws they were making; but it also creates the potential for a greater responsiveness, by the Commissions and by the legal establishment as a whole.

The Commissions are not responsible for investigating individual claims of discrimination: this falls to the Industrial Tribunals, although individuals can seek assistance from the appropriate Commission. However, they are empowered to carry out 'formal investigations' into discrimination in employment, housing, education and the provision of services. This authorization has considerable potential. It is a recognition that discrimination has a long history in our society — so long that in many circumstances it has become invisible — and that positive measures are needed to uncover and tackle it.

Unfortunately, however, a House of Lords ruling in 1984, concerning an investigation proposed by the CRE, severely curtailed the power of both Commissions to conduct formal investigations. The judgment, which was sought by the Prestige Group plc, said that the CRE could not conduct an investigation into a named organisation unless it had definite suspicions that unlawful acts were being committed.

The CRE commented:

> The difficulty this raises is that it is almost impossible for an individual . . . to assemble the comparative evidence necessary to know whether he or she is being discriminated against. Only when the system is looked at as a whole does the existence of discrimination become apparent. (CRE: *Review of the Race Relations Act* 1985.)

This, of course, also holds true in cases of sex discrimination. Race and sex discrimination are deeply embedded in our society and in its very institutions. We therefore consider it necessary that the original powers of both Commissions be reinforced, so that they can conduct the investigations needed to uncover hidden discrimination.

A further weakness in the authority of the Commissions is that they cannot stipulate the changes that should result if an employer has discriminated. In NCCL's comments on the (then) Sex Discrimination Bill in 1975, we proposed that the EOC should be able to make *binding* recommendations, backed up if necessary by a court order. That proposal was rejected and the result is that the EOC, after conducting a formal investigation, has no power to ensure that the employer's practices are changed. We propose that, at the very least, both the EOC and the CRE should be able to make binding recommendations designed to achieve two aims: first, to ensure that the employer introduces practices and procedures which will reduce the likelihood of unlawful discrimination; and second, to direct the employer to make use of the positive action sections of the present legislation if these are needed to remove disadvantage to women or ethnic minority employees.

Finally, we propose that the EOC's authority to monitor and review the Sex Discrimination and Equal Pay Acts be extended to *all* areas of legislation which affect women at work. At present, for instance, the EOC has no powers to monitor the significant encroachments on women's maternity rights at work which have taken place since they were first set out in the Employment Protection Act of 1975. There have been some extraordinary rulings in relation to sex discrimination and pregnancy: in 1979 a tribunal decided that a claim of unlawful sex discrimination taken by a woman who was dismissed when she became pregnant could not be upheld because there was no man in 'materially similar circumstances'! (Turley *v.* Arding and Hobbs Ltd.) In order to avoid decisions of this kind it is essential that full use is made of the specialist knowledge available. In NCCL's briefing on the 1983 Sex Equality Bill we therefore proposed that the EOC be given powers to review the workings of the Employment Protection (Consolidation) Act 1978, and that it be empowered to assist in legal proceedings under the employment legislation where they are linked to sex discrimination.

Strengthening the Tribunals

Finally, we would like to see certain changes in the administration and scope of the Industrial Tribunals, which have the investigative and judicial responsibility for claims of discrimination. The Tribunals are responsible for a vast range of other employment-related complaints: claims under the Equal Pay, Sex Discrimination and Race Relations Acts form only a tiny proportion of their work.

The tribunals are supposed to be quick, efficient, and most of all informal, so that they are readily accessible to people who have no experience of the law and cannot prepare complicated legal arguments in support of their claims. This is very important, because no legal aid can be awarded to claimants in discrimination tribunals, and unless they can pay for it, they therefore have no access to expert legal advice — let alone representation. However, the supposed informality of the tribunals has become increasingly mythical. Employers *can* afford legal advice and representation, and they generally make full use of it. As well as giving them an original unfair advantage, this inevitably introduces more complexity and jargon into the proceedings, which compounds the problem. NCCL has long argued that legal aid *should* be available to discrimination claimants, and we will continue to press for this.

An additional difficulty is that the Industrial Tribunals are not specialists in discrimination cases: the bulk of their work, as we mentioned, is on wholly different issues, and they therefore have little opportunity to build up the necessary expertise on the anti-discrimination laws and case law. This has resulted in confused and confusing judgments. (See Alice Leonard: *Judging Inequality: Sex Discrimination and Equal Pay Claims in the Industrial Tribunals*, forthcoming from the Cobden Trust.) We therefore consider that specialist Tribunals should be set up just to deal with cases of equal pay, and sex and race discrimination. Members of the Tribunals should be fully trained, both in how to apply the legislation and in how to administer the proceedings so that they are as clear and informal as they were intended to be.

Lastly, we propose that the Tribunals be given greater powers of enforcement. At present they can exact compensatory payments from employers for successful claimants, but they cannot insist that the employer take positive steps to avoid repetitions of the original discrimination. Nor can they recommend that women who have lost their jobs as a result of discrimination be reinstated. We consider that they should have both of these powers. Financial compensation for claimants — particularly at the derisory levels currently being fixed by Tribunals — is no compensation for being denied or losing a job. If reinstatement is impractical, the financial award should reflect much more accurately the real financial losses to the claimant. Similarly, if a Tribunal finds an employer to have unlawfully discriminated, it should be able to specify a comprehensive course of action to be followed by that employer in order to improve the situation. In this way the Tribunals would, like the EOC, be capable of providing much more effective remedies for discrimination.

Further Reading

Women and Employment: a lifetime perspective Martin and Roberts (HMSO, 1984)

The Other Half of Our Future Report on women and training from the Women's National Commission (Cabinet Office, 1984)

Equal at Work Anna Coote (Collins, 1979)

Sex Discrimination in the Labour Market B. Chiplin and P. Solane (Macmillan, 1976)

Schooling for Women's Work R. Dee (RKP, 1980)

Women, Work and Trade Union Organisation J. Hunt and S. Adams (WEA, 1980)

Part Time Workers (Labour Research Department, 1986)

The First Eight Years — A profile of the Equal Pay and Sex Discrimination Tribunals Alice Leonard (EOC, 1985)

Sex Discrimination in Industrial Tribunals Alice Leonard (The Cobden Trust, 1986)

Review of the Race Relations Act 1976: proposals for change (CRE, 1985)

Childcare for All (National Childcare Campaign, 1985)

Women's Rights and the EEC: a guide for women in the UK (Rights of Women Europe, 1983)

Women's Pay: Claiming Equal Value (Labour Research Department, 1986)

Women's Employment Rights: a guide for trade unionists (Labour Research Department, 1984)

Women at Work L. Mackie and P. Patullo (Tavistock, 1977)

A Practical Guide to Discrimination Law M. Malone (Grant McIntyre, 1980)

Sex Discrimination Law David Pannick (Clarendon, 1985)

Learning from Uncle Sam: Equal Employment Opportunity Programmes David Wainwright (Runnymede, 1980)

The GLC Women's Committee: A Record of Change and Achievement for Women in London (GLC, 1986)

Anti-Sexist Initiatives in ILEA Schools A. Coulter (ILEA, 1983)

Women in the Labour Market (TUC Women's Advisory Committee, 1983)

Women in Management C. Cooper and M. Davidson (Heinemann, 1984)

Women and Harassment at Work Natalie Hadjifotiou (Pluto, 1983)

Your Job in the Eighties Ursula Huws (Pluto, 1982)

Through the Bureaucratic Maze: Managing Equal Opportunity Programmes David Wainwright (Runnymede, 1983)

Positive Action for Women Workers (NALGO, 1983)

Invisible Women: the Schooling Scandal Dale Spender (Writers and Readers, 1982)

Publications from NCCL's Women's Rights Unit

Amending the Equality Laws Cash Scorer and Ann Sedley (NCCL, 1983)

Sexual Harassment at Work Ann Sedley and Melissa Benn (NCCL, 1984)

Maternity Rights for Women at Work Jean Coussins, Lyn Durward and Ruth Evans (NCCL, 1986)

Part-time Workers Need Full-time Rights Ann Sedley (NCCL, 1983)

The Equality Report — A survey of the first year of the Equal Pay and Sex Discrimination Acts Jean Coussins (NCCL, 1976)

Women's Rights - the Penguin Guide Revised Edition. Anna Coote and Tess Gill (Penguin, 1981)

No More Peanuts — A look at the equal pay legislation Jo Morris (NCCL, 1983)

NCCL fights for Women's Rights

The **National Council for Civil Liberties** has fought against all kinds of discrimination since 1934. In 1973 the Rights for Women Unit was set up to defend and extend women's rights. Our current work includes:

Making equality laws work

We have fought important test cases to determine how far the Sex Discrimination and Equal Pay Acts can help women. We have submitted detailed proposals for amending both Acts to make them more effective, and have assisted in drafting a Private Members Bill to change the law.

Positive Action

It is now clear that even if the laws were amended, they would have only limited use. We have set up experimental Positive Action projects at different kinds of workplaces, to show that *real* equal opportunities, negotiated between union and management, mean much more than neutral non-discrimination policies.

Part-time workers' rights

Eighty per cent of part-time workers are women and they operate in a low-paid underprivileged ghetto. We are fighting to improve their conditions of employment and the range of work available to them – aiming to make a shorter working week an attractive and realistic option for *all* parents.

Tax and Social Security

We have led the campaign to end discrimination in the tax and social security systems.

Maternity Rights

We publish the only guide to the rights of pregnant women at work. By 1983, it had sold more than 20,000 copies.

Immigration and Nationality

The NCCL campaigns for a non-sexist, non-racist law and practice. In 1974 we won the campaign to restore to women their right to live in their own country, whatever their husband's nationality. This right has been taken again from some women and we are continuing our fight.

Abortion

We have always opposed any restriction to the 1967 Abortion Act. Together with ALRA, we set up the women's right to choose campaign.

Sexual Harassment at Work

We believe that sexual harassment can constitute unlawful sexual discrimination. We published the first guide to sexual harassment at work and have assisted in many cases and campaigns.

The 28-year-old age limit for direct entry into the Civil Service meant that Belinda Price, who was returning to work after looking after her children, could not get a job in the Executive Officer Grade. NCCL argued that the age bar constituted indirect discrimination and the Civil Service has now had to change its entry requirements to comply with the law.

Brenda Clarke and Sandra Powell both worked part-time in a factory and were made redundant before the full-timers, under an agreement made between the union and management. NCCL took the case up and argued that if full-timers are given more favourable treatment than part-timers it was indirect discrimination as most part-timers are women. The EAT ruled that this agreement constituted gross discrimination. Both Brenda and Sandra were reinstated and many of their colleagues, also sacked, received compensation.

Jane C. wanted to train to be a nurse. She was told she had to work full-time for six months before she would be accepted for training as the Area Health Authority wanted proof she had proper childcare arrangements. We encouraged her to join a union and contacted COHSE who immediately sorted out the problem for her.

As a result of enquiries from women who had been called for jury service but refused adequate child-care allowances, NCCL took up the issue of sex discrimination in jury allowances. We have now won recognition of the right of women to claim full reimbursement for child-care expenses while on jury service.

This is just some of our work, and it all costs money. For our regular income, we depend on donations from supporters. You can help us by making a donation by banker's order to the Women's Rights Fund, and receive a regular newsletter keeping you up to date with our work.

**RIGHTS FOR WOMEN UNIT,
NATIONAL COUNCIL FOR CIVIL LIBERTIES
21 Tabard Street, London SE1 4LA**

Banker's Order Form

To: (Your Bank)   From: (Your name & address)

BANK _____   NAME _____

ADDRESS _____   ADDRESS _____

ACCOUNT NO _____   POSTCODE _____

Please pay to the account of: **NCCL, Williams & Glyn's Bank, 25 Millbank, London SWIP 4RB** (Sorting code: 15 30 00), Account number: **71186884**; PLEASE QUOTE REFERENCE: **Women's Rights Fund**.

The Sum of (words): _____ In Figures: _____

on the _____ day of _____ . (month) 19 , and every year/month* on £15 a year – whichever is most

the same day until otherwise notified.   *delete as appropriate

SIGNED _____ DATE _____

Will YOU Join the Women's Rights Fund?

We cannot continue our current level of activity unless we substantially increase the size of the Women's Rights Fund. We want to continue *and expand* our work. We think we have made good use of the Fund so far. We are certain there's a greater demand for our work than we are able to meet at present.

All you have to do is to fill in the Banker's Order form for £2 a month or £15 a year – whichever is most convenient to you. Give more if you can afford it! You will then receive from us a regular newsletter, keeping you up-to-date with our work.

WOMEN'S RIGHTS

Women Won't Benefit £1.95 **NEW**
Hilary Land and *Sue Ward.* The impact of the social security review on women.
NCCL 1986. ISBN 0 946088 26 8

The Rape Controversy £1.50 **NEW**
Melissa Benn, Anna Coote and *Tess Gill.* Up-to-date in February 1986, this new edition looks at the prevailing myths about rape, the facts that refute them and the need to support and extend the work done to help women who have been raped. It examines how the law works and looks at police procedure.
NCCL 1986. ISBN 0 946088 23 3.

Positive Action for Women £4.95 **NEW**
Paddy Stamp and *Sadie Robarts.* An examination of the achievements in the positive action field over the past ten years, with recommendations for the future.
NCCL 1986. ISBN 0 946088 25 X.

Maternity Rights at Work £1.50 **NEW**
Ruth Evans, Lyn Durward and *Jean Coussins.* Updated to cover the latest legislation, this practical guide explains how women can get maternity benefits and leave. Invaluable reading for any woman who wants to return to work after having a baby.
NCCL 1986. ISBN 0 946088 24 1. Forthcoming

Maternity Rights Handbook £4.95
Ruth Evans and *Lyn Durward.* Compiled by the Maternity Alliance, this book covers pregnancy and childbirth, rights at work, childcare, family law, child health and maternity benefits.
Penguin

No More Peanuts £2.50
Jo Morris. This book looks at why the Equal Pay Act is not working. It demonstrates why equal value is such an important concept for women's equality, by examining the low-pay trap, job segregation, how skills are defined and why women's jobs are usually valued less than men's. It is illustrated throughout and specially designed with examples and role-play exercises for use on education courses, in women's groups and trade unions.
NCCL 1983. ISBN 0 946088 08 X

Judging Women 95p
Polly Pattullo. The law has always been biased against women. It defines them as second-class citizens, reinforces myths and popular prejudice and patronises women who practise it. This pamphlet looks at the history of women's experience at the hands of the law, at some of the absurdities pronounced by judges and the inequalities perpetuated in the law.
NCCL 1984. ISBN 0 946088 07 1

Amending the Equality Laws 95p
Catherine Scorer and *Ann Sedley.* Argues the need for radical reform of the equality legislation which has done little to alter reality for most women. It brings together all the major criticisms and suggestions for change.
NCCL 1983. ISBN 0 946088 04 7

Sexual Harassment at Work 95p
Ann Sedley and *Melissa Benn.* Sexual harassment is now recognised as a major problem facing women at work. This book looks at how comon the problem is, how women are organising to oppose it and what trade unions can do.
NCCL 1982. ISBN 0 946088 00 4

The Unequal Breadwinner 60p
Ruth Lister and *Leo Wilson.* Shows the way in which many women are penalised when they are the main breadwinners in their families – in taxation, unemployment benefit, family income supplement and pensions.
NCCL 1976. ISBN 0 901108 57 X

Women's Rights – The Penguin Guide £3.95
Anna Coote and *Tess Gill.* The complete guide to women's rights. Revised edition.
Penguin 1981. ISBN 0 14 046532 4

Battered Women and the New Law £1.50
Anna Coote and *Tess Gill.* Contains information and advice about how to cope with domestic violence.
NCCL and Inter-Action. 1979. ISBN 0 904571 19 X

Shift Work Swindle 60p
Jean Coussins. The argument against the repeal of protective legislation for women in factories.
NCCL 1979. ISBN 0 091108 81 2

Income Tax and Sex Discrimination 85p
Patricia Hewitt. A practical guide to income tax, highlighting the injustices which still face women.
NCCL 1979. ISBN 0 901108 84 7

Part-Time Workers need Full-Time Rights 95p
Ann Sedley. This shows how part-time workers, most of whom are women, are discriminated against. With a complete guide to their rights.
NCCL 1983. ISBN 0 901108 61 8

The Equality Report £1.20
Jean Coussins. A detailed survey of the first year of the Equal Pay and the Sex Discrimination Acts.
NCCL 1976. ISBN 0 901108 61 8

Order form: Please indicate below the quantity and titles you require:

	Qty.	£		Qty.	£
Women Won't Benefit		£1.95	Sexual Harassment at Work		95p
The Rape Controversy		£1.50	The Unequal Breadwinner		60p
Positive Action for Women		£4.95	Women's Rights – The Penguin Guide		£3.95
Maternity Rights at Work		£1.50	Battered Women and the New Law		£1.50
Maternity Rights Handbook		£4.95	Shift Work Swindle		60p
No More Peanuts		£2.50	Income Tax and Sex Discrimination		85p
Judging Women		95p	Part-Time Workers Need Full-Time Rights		95p
Amending the Equality Laws		95p	The Equality Report		£1.20

Postage and Packing: Total up to £1.95 – **25p** Total £2.00 – £4.95 – **40p**
Total £5.00 – £9.95 **75p** Total over £10.00 – **FREE**

Total value of your order   £ _____
Add for postage and packing £ _____
Total value of remittance   £ _____

NAME _____

ADDRESS _____

All overseas orders will be sent by surface mail.
For airmail please add 50% to your remittance.
Please remit as a sterling cheque if possible.

NCCL Rights for Women Unit, 21 Tabard Street, London SE1 4LA.